Dear Tiny

great meeting you.
Always keep your light of
excellence shining.

Yours in health,

Graham.

4D Leadership

MASTER THE 4 D'S OF SUCCESS
AND LIVE YOUR DREAMS

FOREWORD
BY BOB PROCTOR

DR HISHAM ABDALLA

Dr®HISHAM

www.4dleadership.com

4D LEADERSHIP
MASTER THE 4 D'S OF SUCCESS AND LIVE YOUR DREAMS

1ST EDITION PUBLISHED IN 2012 BY
LASERGENIUS CREATIVE PUBLISHING
WWW.4DLEADERSHIP.COM

PUBLISHED WITH THE ASSISTANCE OF
PUBLICIOUS PTY LTD
WWW.PUBLICIOUS.COM.AU

CATALOGUING-IN-PUBLICATION INFORMATION AVAILABLE ON REQUEST

AUTHOR: DR HISHAM ABDALLA
TITLE: 4D LEADERSHIP
ISBN: 978-0-9873726-0-4

ALSO AVAILABLE AS AN EBOOK: 978-0-9873726-1-1

PROFESSIONAL EDIT BY MARIA D'MARCO,
WWW.TIGERXGLOBAL.COM

COVER AND LAYOUT DESIGN BY TRENDS DIGITAL INTERNATIONAL
WWW.TRENDSIDEAS.COM

BOOK LAYOUT BY PUBLICIOUS PTY LTD

Dedication:

This book is dedicated to all the people I serve and those who serve me.

Special dedications are given:

To my mother, the person who believed in me even before I was born, and who taught me that a parent's greatest pride is having their children's achievements surpass their own.

To my wife, my love, and the rock that I stand on. Without her love, dedication, and unconditional support while managing our home and businesses, I would never have the achievements I have today.

To my daughter Noor, the brilliance in my life and the light of my soul. She is for whom I live and will die trying to leave a legend she would be proud to follow.

To my sisters Shireen and Nisreen, my nieces Sara and Yasmeen, and my nephew Mohamed, for their love and unconditional trust.

To David my friend and coach, for his belief in my dreams. And to all my other mentors and teachers over the years from whom I draw inspiration.

To my friends, my guests, my colleagues, my students, and my great team who have gifted me their trust and made me a leader by their permission.

It is never one's own choice to lead others; it is their choice to be led by one's actions and character. That is a responsibility and honor I take very seriously.

Above all, I dedicate this to The One God who created me and gave me the gifts of talent, mind, tongue, and hands to be able to add value to the world.

In gratitude and appreciation for His gifts.

Contents

Bob Proctor

Over the past 50 years, I have conducted seminars and programs worldwide helping people to understand the wondrous potential of their marvelous mind. After reading the principles Dr. Hisham brilliantly shares with us in his 4D Leadership book, it is obvious to me that he solidly understands the message of achieving our greatest potential in life.

We live in a world filled with an abundance of knowledge and It seems that every day another book is being released on the subject of success. But, are the authors really congruent with their messages? With complete confidence, I can say that Hisham is!

Frankly, it is nice to find such a powerfully informative book where the author has tested his approach and determined it effective before sharing it with us. Personally, I've read thousands of books and have a great sense of knowing those with the potential to make a powerful impact.

With this in mind, I can say that the wisdom and guidance offered in this book have the potential to impact you in a very positive way.

As you work your way through the pages of this book, you will discover the value of time and that what you do with your time will make all the difference in your life. You will reach a greater understanding of what you can control and you will also become aware of those aspects of life over which we have no control. I truly believe you will be amazed at the impact you can have on your own future with a little extra thought and the application of Dr. Hisham's advice.

It all begins with awareness. You must be willing to look anew at things in your world and become consciously aware of the infinitely powerful being that you are.

It is important to mention that even though Dr. Hisham's book title includes the word "leadership", the content in this book truly does apply to everyone. Whether you are currently in a role of leadership or not, at some point in your life, leadership is something you need to understand and grasp. Dr Hisham's 4D principles help you to perceive that you are the leader of your own life, and the sooner you take charge, the sooner you will be experiencing the extraordinary life you were meant to live.

In Napoleon Hill's classic book "Think & Grow Rich" it is stated: "Every person who wins in any undertaking must be willing to burn his ships and cut all sources of retreat. Only by so doing can one be sure of maintaining that state of mind known as a BURNING DESIRE TO WIN, essential to success."

I suspect you have a desire to win since you've picked up this book. And, winning is what you will do when you heed the messages contained within.

Invest some time to truly think about what you want. Do you know what you desire?

Permit me to suggest that you consciously think about your answer to this question as you go through this book – and then, make an irrevocable decision to become all you are capable of being. Stay focused and think about what you want and only about what you want.

What do you really desire?

Dr. Hisham speaks of "decision, dedication and action". Make the decision now to be all you are capable of being and dedicate your life to it. You will be glad you did.

You were designed with greatness in mind. Now is the time to take action and make your life a masterpiece.

Bob Proctor

The Fourth Dimension: TIME

I envisage a world full of happy, healthy, and gratified people living in collaborative harmony. Such a society would, however, only come about through empowering individuals with properly applied knowledge, elevated awareness, and enduring experiences that inspire growth.

We all know that we live in a 3-D (three dimensional) world. The awareness of 3-D and its impact on our senses are heightened by today's technology. From 3-D movies and 3-D TV to computer 3-D design and games, we are all becoming much more aware of the intensity of a 3-D compared to a 2-D experience.

In real life, we constantly see and interact with everything around us as 3 dimensional objects. This is because of our innate spatial recognition of length, width and depth, but there is also the 4th dimension that we are all bound by, which is not physically somatic: Time.

Albert Einstein's theories changed how science looks at the world and designated Time as the fourth dimension. In Einstein's Special Relativity, time behaves astonishingly like the three dimensions of space where distances shorten and length contracts as speed increases.

Time expands as speed increases.

So far as we know, time goes only in one direction, forward. We do not know how to go back in time. That is a very important fact to keep in mind when you go through life, there is no way back in time, only forward. Time ticks into infinity, with or without our involvement. We are irrelevant to time, but it is relevant to us.

Our variable speed relates us to the constant of time.

How does the 4th Dimension of Time relate to everyday life and success or leadership in particular?

Well, the fact is, we have limited time on this earth as physical individuals. One can never know how long he or she will live. We can only control our actions and the results we achieve during our finite time in this mortal world. Therefore, it helps to know that the 4th dimension "Time", as it relates to the universe around us, can work in our favour or can work against us, depending on the thoughts and actions we apply to it.

For example, if I focus harder and move faster towards my target, the time it takes to get there will be shortened, right? So, if you want to achieve many goals during your finite life on this earth, you had best take less time to get to each, so as to achieve as many goals as possible within the total time allocated to you.

Time, like the Universe, existed before human beings and will outlast us. It is as infinite as the Divine Intelligence that creates, rules, and permeates the Universe. Time is not something we can control or even manage, but we can control our own flight path through that dimension to achieve as much as we decide to achieve within a given period.

To lead your own life to maximize the benefits to yourself, your family and the world around you, during and after your time on this earth, is true leadership.

I call this living to leave a legend.

Legends of a person's goodwill, contributions, teachings, and inspirations shared will outlast their finite 3-D existence in this world and transcend to the 4th dimension of Time, impacting the future beyond their physical presence.

The challenge of our Time

The goal of this pragmatic book is to share with you the real life implications of applying my "4D's of Leadership Success" in a 4-dimensional world to help you quickly achieve and continually sustain leadership in a life of personal success, joy and fulfilment.

Through the study of the wisdom revealed in my religion and other religions, in science, and in the wisdom of past and present thinkers and philosophers, plus mentors and coaches, I have evolved my simple theory of 4D Leadership.

And then, I went out and proved that it works – for anyone - in real life.

The challenge in today's fast-changing world, full of abundance and opportunity, is overcoming the contradicting messages of fear propaganda, pre-emptive wars, crisis, and those who believe the end of the world is near.

Ignorance, apathy, and fear work in concert to control the global mind set. This is living in the dark, a state of low to no energy or being. Yet, light always outshines the dark, because it is a higher level of energy and being. The light of awareness, hope, inspiration, and faith in yourself, your life, and your contribution to the world must prevail if we, the human race, are to continue co-existing and evolving in a new dimension.

I am finishing this book at a point in time where the fear mob is proclaiming that the end of all is December 21st. 2012 - and for so many reasons and prophecies, but mainly, because the 5000 year Mayan calendar ends on this date!

I cannot believe or accept this point of doom. The current levels of mankind's emotional awareness and physical progress promise a new level of interaction with our 4D world at a much higher speed of travel through time and space. What happened is that ancient wisdom and awareness could only foresee this far, because we don't know what infinity is or how to interact with it.

From here onwards, it is you and I and all of us who will create a new time calendar for our new world future.

This future is for a new world order where singularity with our higher consciousness and innovative intelligence is achieved. The world will not end in December 2012. A whole new world will begin, if we all care enough to create it.

As humans, we are the Supreme Beings of this world, but not of the Universe. It is in our hands, minds, and hearts to create or destroy our world on this Earth.

Whether it is our individual spheres of influence or the whole wide world, the point is the same. Until we all believe that we can and should do better with our given gifts, talents, knowledge, and capabilities to serve our time and our species, the world may as well just end now.

The difference lies in our collaborative respect for each other, the creative genius that the Creator gifted us with, and our unique ability to grow cognisant awareness and make better choices. The vision starts now and the action has to follow with an absolute determination to evolve and not dissolve.

Let's do that together, create foresight to write up a vision calendar for our world to become better and better.

This book is not about business success, entrepreneurial leadership, family unity, cultural evolution, human service, or even love or world peace. It is about all of these things and more, starting at the individual level. It is about people taking responsibility for their own lives, actions, and circumstances, while becoming personal leaders of their own destiny.

It is time to stop giving up the power of leadership to those few at the so-called top, while the rest of us follow.

The world is changing and will continue to change. It can only improve though, one person at a time. It starts with you and me.

_____

My Fight

I have a fight in me. It's a fight against human ignorance, apathy, intolerance and tolerance. It's a fight for knowledge, awareness, caring, and **acceptance** of everyone else on this planet.

Our fight is not with the world, our fight is within each of us to grow and lead a better life that inspires humankind.

Our common enemy is fear and our survival-reactive response to it: fight or flight.

Once we beat the causes of fear, as I will show you in this book, we are not worried about survival anymore, so we no longer simply react to life. We are freed to consciously act and lead better and better lives.

Our fight should have a higher meaning, so let's choose a fight that empowers rather than denigrates humanity.

I invite you to take up this challenge with me. Read this book and start living as a personal leader of your own success story, no matter where you are in your life today. Then, inspire others by joining in the conversation on the 4D Leadership website www.4dleadership.com or on our Facebook page. Instructions will be on the website. We will run contests for the best 4D leader success stories that can win you recognition.

No matter what your start status may be, whether you have a lot of goals to achieve, are successful in some or many areas of your life, or are already at the top of your game in life - read this book, share your video, and find others around you who can benefit by learning and understanding the 4D's.

Let's create true freedom and peace within, which will express as freedom and peace without.

Let's join together to make this world better and better.

Dr. Hisham

Life & Lessons

My father's death was a tipping point for me, and also for writing this book.

At the time, I was 28 years old and in the middle of constructing my life's dream, the Laser lifeCARE Institute. I remember every moment of the ordeal of losing my father as if it were yesterday. It all started the 22nd of December 2005.

My father had slipped into coma after a bad fall while walking unassisted in the hospital in Auckland. He had been admitted for constant vertigo and dizziness, and then dismissed without diagnosis. I had come to pick him up after work and found that his head was bleeding – blood covering his pillow. I was very angry when I learned what had happened, but there was no use trying to assign blame - all we could think of was how to help him.

I spent all the next day by his side while scans were done for brain hemorrhages, trying to find the cause of his coma and if it could be abated. Unfortunately, it soon became obvious that his end was near.

In this turmoil, the shock of losing my dad dropped me into deep sorrow. I worried for him as his soul's finite time on this earth was ticking quickly away.

I didn't know how he felt inside, but I was certain that although his body was still, his mind was frantically questioning. Is this the end? How can I tell everybody whom I love that I do, before I go? Did I make right any wrongs that I have done? Did I pay back all my debts? Did I ask for forgiveness and apologize for anything I may have said that had upset anyone? Did I fulfill my duties to my family, my soul and my God? Did I pray enough and repent for forgiveness from The God Almighty? Where will I, the soul of me, go after leaving this mortal body and world? Is this the end?

I knew he was afraid, because as he lay in bed, I saw a tear roll from each of his shut eyes. I cried at the sight and then suddenly stopped. All the medical science I had studied, and the religious and spiritual learning I had gone through in my life came forward, reminding me that the mind is always aware as long as the soul is in the body.

Even while my father's heart beat its last beats and his blood made its last circuits through his vessels, I knew that if I spoke to him, he would hear me.

I gently put my arm across his chest and leaned close to his ear. I told him that I knew he was still with us and was afraid. I told him that I loved him - that we all loved him. I told him I was sorry for anytime I had ever upset him and I asked for his forgiveness. I had never spoken to my dad like that before.

It is strange how we can change in the face of adversity.

I told him I would pray for him as long as I lived, to ask The One God to bless him and have mercy on his soul when he meets Him. I kept reminding him to pray, repent and ask for forgiveness every minute. I promised him that I would fight hard for my dreams; to make up for his many unfulfilled dreams. I told him that I was grateful that he is my dad.

In the evening of the next day, while we were around him praying, I again leaned in close to speak to him and this time I had my sister, who was overseas at the time, on the phone at his other ear. Suddenly, he started to shake vigorously and his eyes opened wide in horror. He must have seen the angel of death and that is no easy sight, as the Holy books all tell us. I kept holding him and praying in his ear. I reminded him of the last proclamation words he had to say in his heart before he could say no more. And then, he lay still and stopped breathing. His eyes were relaxed, but glazed and he had a small smile on his face.

I believe we helped him pass over in peace. I hugged him and said goodbye, for now.

I have to wonder what thoughts will go through my mind when my time comes. In the meantime, I had a renewed commitment to myself, my dad, and to the world to do even better than I had dreamed of doing before - and to share my experiences with anyone willing to listen. I wanted to see the world become better and better and decided to transcribe my journey, as my story progressed.

The book

I started writing this book on my 34th birthday, the 1st of January 2011 (1.1.11).

While the seed of the book was planted years ago, the roots had to grow and set in first. Then the plant had to break ground and the fruits of that seed had to develop and mature before they could be harvested. Time had to pass. With perseverance in nurturing that seed, the outcome manifested as reality. People more readily relate to ideas and theoretical concepts that they can physically see, touch and interact with. That is why one must wait for the fruit to develop.

I had reached a financially secure position in my life, having become a millionaire at the time, and felt I could finally justify putting my long held thoughts and ideas into a book that might motivate and benefit others.

I had also wanted to prove that my concept actually worked in the real world before I shared it. Integrity is essential in everything that I do, as a medical professional, an educator, a mentor, and now as a writer. Trust is all I've got to sell and I can't afford to short sell on that - nor do I ever intend to. Therefore, everything that I say I did or do, must be backed up with evidence. I must take responsibility for the reactions and consequences of my words and actions as they apply to others.

Every part of my foreword, the telling of my personal story, has a moral and lessons that relate to 4D Leadership and uphold what you will read in the chapters of this book.

There are many little secrets to success, but once you uncover them, they become living reality and not secrets anymore.

Please read on…

A Whole New World

I am the product of today's changing face of the world - a high tech world that moves extremely fast and is interconnected, interdependent and multicultural in every way. The Universe is expanding and our world is following. Our awareness of how to harness the physical bounty of this universe for our own benefit is more evident in the last 100 years than in the total sum of all human history.

I am part of the new breed seen everywhere these days: multi-ethnic, multi-lingual, multi-cultural and multi-colored. This new breed developed world awareness by living in multiple countries and continents and traveling more than most of our ancestors have. This breed is shaped by an interwoven, tech-savvy world that relies on people 'accepting and respecting' others as fellow human beings, rather than merely 'tolerating' or even worse 'denouncing' them because they are 'different'.

I believe in The One God and my religion is a continuation of the other great religions from the same God through holy messengers before. Yet I read, respect, and accept all other spiritual beliefs and non-beliefs.

Freedom to choose a belief relies on mutual acceptance and respect. As long as we do not harm one another for any reason, debating our beliefs and views on life, our spiritualties and cultures is productive for the evolution of humankind and the mental growth of individuals.

For human kind to evolve in unity, it is best to invite others into our world, our religions, and our cultures through living, being and conveying the best of that. Unfortunately many individuals deter others by expressing the worst human traits possible, then blaming it on their religion, culture, social status or background.

"Mental valor is being satisfied that you're right, without feeling the need to prove somebody else wrong."

The time of empires, superior races, monocultures and strict borders is long gone. Anyone doubting this need just look around with open eyes and mind, take it in, accept it, and make the best out of the new world opportunities. Yeah baby, it's a whole new world.

Specific examples of the success of this new mixed and intertwined breed abound, but one person that is most prominent in representing the above description is President Barack Obama.

Everything in life is just what it is

I give out the facts of my life only to impress upon you that what happens to us just is.

Life - and whatever may happen in it - is not good or bad, it just is.

What you make out of the circumstances of your life and the gifts that you were given depends upon your attitude towards life, what you learn from these circumstances, and what you decide to do with that knowledge.

What you do with what you have learned, determines your value to the world. We don't get rewarded, paid or appreciated for what we know, but rather for <u>what we do</u> with what we know.

For example, I was born on the 1st of January 1977. Now, 1.1.77 has a symmetric look to it and some have even told me it's a lucky number. But - is it lucky? And does a certain number being considered as "lucky" mean anything? I think it's just a number – a number I didn't even choose. I tried it as lotto numbers, but never won. So much for lucky!

My beginning in life was being born in Khartoum, Sudan, of multi-ethnic roots in an area where all people shared the same culture, but different religions. Our Coptic neighbors, who owned and filled up most of the apartments in the building we lived in, were at all our festivities and we were at all theirs. We didn't even know there was any difference and really, there wasn't.

I have not traced my family tree, but do know that my bloodlines are of Egyptian, Arabic, African, and Turkish lineage. I do not care if this is good or bad, it just is.

My mother had an Egyptian mother and African father with Arabian roots. Both had mixed blood themselves. My father had an Egyptian father from Aswan in the south of Egypt, with roots back to the Pharaohs, and a Sudanese mother who had Turkish roots.

I never met my paternal grandparents. My father's mother died when he was a boy and his father later on. His grandmother and aunt brought him up. His was a large family and that shaped my father's views of the world. He went on to specialize in leather and hide biochemistry in Egypt and England.

My mother's parents split when she was in University studying to be a doctor. She went on to specialize as an ophthalmic surgeon. Hers was a well off family, as her father was a merchant in African goods. All this shaped my mother's views on life.

When I was three, and my sister almost five, our parents decided to move to Abu Dhabi, United Arab Emirates, to give us a better future and education. We attended a Catholic school run by Lebanese nuns.

As a Muslim in a Catholic private school, with a huge multi-ethnic and multi-religious mix, it shaped my first years in life. Respect for others' beliefs and diversity was 'the norm'. Beginning in kindergarten, we studied Arabic, English, and French. I am grateful to my parents for starting us out on such a diverse path for learning.

My grandmother looked after my sister and I most of the time, as my parents worked hard to build their careers and bring in the goods of life. She was not a mainstream educated woman, but was nevertheless very wise and exceptionally nurturing. One of her everlasting impressions on me was her saying "always speak good, and if you have nothing nice to say, be quiet". God bless her soul, she passed away in 2002.

We were not a rich family, but had a good middle class life without deprivation. I am grateful for that, too.

What I learned from my parents, by example, are the two main concepts I have lived by through my life so far: continuous hunger for education and ethical hard work.

What I learned from their mistakes, again by example and observation, is that being a hardworking, well-educated professional will never guarantee you a good life long term, and especially when you retire.

No government, enterprise, or company can ever guarantee you a lifelong job opportunity. This is particularly so if you rely solely on your physical presence, ability, skills, and knowledge to produce an income.

Investing, money management, and business ideas were not my parent's forte and it showed later in their lives. They lost their life savings by trusting everything to a wealthy family member who got himself in deep trouble with bad investments. He lost all his capital, his family, plus all of the money entrusted to him by other people like my parents, and spent years in jail regretting it all.

Lesson #1: Sound judgment of how and where you invest your money and learning about the world of business are critical skills. These were lessons I learned from my parents' honest mistakes – lessons that shaped my decisions in life.

My parents' savior in their later years, emotionally and physically, was their unconditional investment in us, their children. Our education and development always came as top priority for them and that paid off in more ways than one.

After finishing our Cambridge University International General Certificate of Secondary Education (IGCSE) exams, my sister and I went together to study medicine/dentistry at Charles University in the Czech Republic. I was 14 and my sister was 16. We were the youngest in class and I was the youngest in the University's recorded history to enter the pre-med school and later was the youngest to graduate as a doctor at 21.

Was that luck?

No. I imagine it was the persistent hard work from my parents, based on our abilities, to push us through school years with high achievements. Getting us through the 4th dimension – Time – as quickly as possible was their goal. They didn't think of that dimension as I am writing of it here, but subconsciously, that's what they did.

My sister Shireen and I possessed the mental ability to achieve what we ultimately achieved, but without a plan or the intent to develop our abilities, we would never have gotten anywhere.

This is a very important point.

Lesson #2: Potential just is and always abundant. Yet it never evolves into results until we realize it, nourish it, and apply it with passion and persistence.

Being only 14, I was both teased and applauded for being the "kid" in University. With this pro and con being handed out by both students and teachers. So, how did I take it? I thought it was great to be noticed and decided that nothing could make me feel discriminated against or judged, unless I allowed it. I took everything as a compliment, regardless of how the other party said or meant it. Eventually, everyone around me learned to accept the reality of me being there and proving myself. I enjoyed the interaction my youthful circumstance created and took that opportunity to learn to speak Czech fluently, quickly becoming a translator for colleagues.

Lesson #3: I chose a positive, affirming reaction and the world responded gradually. I wasn't aware at the time that I was subconsciously applying the Law of Attraction.

Acceptance

I applied the above approach to things that happened in my everyday life during our time in what used to be called Czechoslovakia. It was 1991; just 2 years after the Velvet Revolution and the fall of communist walls and we were the very first group of foreign, private paying students who came to study in English. Some people treated us with excitement and intrigue, some with fear.

I call discrimination and racism fear, because that's what it is.

Fear of the unknown makes us want to avoid it, push it away or attack it. The more we know about something or someone, the less we are afraid and therefore we do not react with that primitive survival mechanism. We become more accepting, understanding and cognitive in our behavior when we are not afraid of what or who is in front of us.

It became apparent to me that in spite of superficial differences in skin color, physical features, and cultural or spiritual backgrounds, shared experiences break down the walls of fear.

So it was our duty, as the new arrivals, to teach the people we came in contact with about ourselves, while respecting their values in their own country. Our behavior expressed who we were and the more love and laughter we put out, the more we were accepted. Soon we were familiar, normal and not feared. Discrimination faded away, but we had to actively create these circumstances; it didn't just happen.

From my immersions I've learned that you will find some people who are fanatical zealots all over the world. They exist in every culture, country, and religion - and they do not want to change. Thankfully, such closed-minded individuals are a minority in the population. The rest of the population consists of everyday people who share more commonalities with the rest of the world than differences, and they accept that.

We all need to socialize, learn, grow, love and be loved, and be appreciated. Once we see that 'others' are just like us from the inside, we need not fear them and we won't discriminate against them. If we treat people as individuals, doing good or bad, and judge that individual behavior, rather than grouping people as all good or all bad because they seem different – our world would be a more peaceful place.

I know from experiencing the world, that when more people dissolve fear through knowledge and acceptance, we will have fewer wars, crime, hate, and judgment. Without the burden of prejudice, we will enjoy more love, peace, and prosperity.

"If I accept the world as you _and_ I, rather than you _or_ I, we could all win. Acceptance of others is the key, not tolerance."

Dr. Hisham

Persistence

In 1998, I was 21 years old and had graduated with honours as a Medical University Doctor of Stomatology (equivalent to Doctor of Dental Medicine in the USA). Shortly after, my fiancée, Marta, and I moved to New Zealand. Soon after that, we got married in Fiji, in a private ceremony in a small chapel amidst palm trees on top of a beautiful hill overlooking the Pacific Ocean.

I had planned to sit the New Zealand Dental Council Exam to register as a dentist over the next year and a half and during that time, I had to study and earn money for the exams and for living.

My first job in New Zealand was a 3-month stint as the attendant on the "graveyard" shift at a Shell petrol station. I was not going to sit at home and whine that I couldn't work in my profession or in my hobby as a DJ, and definitely wasn't going to wait around for opportunity to knock. I never gave up on my intent to pursue what I had come to New Zealand to do, but until I reached that point, I had to work and not complain.

I continued to give out my limited CV to dental clinics all over Auckland in an attempt to find an assisting or temp job. I needed such a job in order to become familiar with the systems and methods of my profession in this part of the world until I sat my Board exams. Finally, I was able to get two separate one-week temp jobs, although it meant working overnight at the Shell station, then a quick early morning shower, to arrive at my temp job by 8 am. I only slept a few hours in the afternoon each day.

Was it tiring? Yes. Was I pleased that I was on track? Absolutely.

After the Shell station job, I worked with my wife in a print-finishing factory. She spoke very little English and was homesick. Marta had given up her familiar environment back home in Czech, her lovely apartment, her family and friends, and a very secure job to follow me to New Zealand - and work in a factory. It wasn't much like a fairytale dream!

All I could do at the time was promise her that our future would be very different and that I needed time to work my plan and create that reality. She trusted me and patiently, but sadly, endured those years while she learned English and integrated within our new environment.

Nothing was real except in my heart. It was all just a dream and a strong desire to do better. No one else could see it, yet my wife and family believed in me.

That was all I needed, plus my 4D's.

Continuous action and determination to accomplish a dream have to take their time, before manifesting as results.

Then came a temp hygienist job for one day a week at Downtown Dental Surgery, which was in Auckland CBD on the waterfront. I was still working at the factory, as well as attending dental, medical, and business seminars, reading and listening to personal development programs, and studying for my Dental Board exams.

During this time, some of the great influences on my thinking were Jim Rohn, Anthony Robbins, Dr. Deepak Chopra and Bob Proctor.

I deeply identified with Bob's picture of the mind and the psycho-cybernetics of self-belief, success, leadership, and the Laws of the Universe as they applied to real life. His perspectives enhanced my pre-existing awareness that I was born rich. Quotes such as, "What we are is God's gift to us. What we become is our gift to God." resonated in total harmony with my understanding of my religion. I understood that I had been subconsciously doing just that, using my God-given gifts to the best of my ability to give back. And now that I was more consciously aware of it, I could enhance it even more. Thank you Bob.

I also took great interest in the lives of stimulating people that made a difference to the world, like Nelson Mandela, Gandhi, mother Theresa and Muhammad Ali.

Different people in different parts of the world at different times, all inspiring us with their persistent commitment to their dreams, despite adversity.

My sister followed a path similar to mine, working smaller jobs while studying, and then getting married. She had her first child the year I took the exams, and so took them the year following.

Risk

My father joined us in New Zealand, but he became ill with congestive heart failure, soon after his arrival, enduring multiple surgeries. These events shattered his dream of gaining employment in leather and hide processing in New Zealand.

LESSON #4: My father's experience revealed that you should never wait to pursue your dream, for the future is unknown. The present is all you can control, in hopes of creating a better future. Look after your health actively and never take it for granted.

My sister Shireen and I looked after our father and our younger sister, who was still at school, while my mother remained in Abu Dhabi. She had to continue working in her field of ophthalmology to pay off the mortgage for their house in New Zealand.

This had not been the plan, but when all their savings vanished with their unfortunate investment decisions, she was no longer able to enjoy early retirement in New Zealand as she had wished.

LESSON #5: From my parent's loss of financial security the importance to get business savvy early, no matter your profession or lack of profession, became clear. Save for retirement and don't rely on one source of income that requires your full physical ability and presence. This is Life Risk Management.

Light-bulb idea

Our daughter Noor (which literally means Light) was born in May 2001. I was 24 and had been working since early 2000 as a full time dentist in the practice where I had been a temp hygienist. In my first year with the practice, I had borrowed $40,000, with great difficulty as a young immigrant with no assets or high earnings history, in order to upgrade my clinic with the latest digital X-ray apparatus, intraoral camera and digital record keeping. Such equipment was available in very few dental clinics at the time, and even today, many dentists here and around the world have not caught on to the digital era yet.

I was planning to buy out one of the partners at the clinic, Dr. Ted, and partner with the two remaining dentists. Ted is a wonderful gentleman. He was very generous and helpful to me, believing in my intent to make a real difference. We are still working together today.

Was that luck - or did I attract him and the situation through my intent and actions? Again, we see the law of attraction in action.

When I came into that practice, there was a laser sitting in the corner of one room collecting dust. I was excited over the find, as it was the same type laser as the one used by one of my Professors in University, and I was one of few students who had been allowed to use it. I asked the partners if I could clean this Nd:YAG laser up and use it. They were delighted at the idea. The laser had been sold to them in 1991 for over $100,000 dollars, with a lot of hype about its capabilities, but no training! It had been very disappointing and a huge waste.

This opportunity to make something from such waste was a trigger point for me.

Light-bulb Idea:

Where do people get advanced training on new technology and advances within their industry or profession? What if it is not something that is standard teaching in universities yet? Who pioneers and develops the uses of new technology further, once it has been invented? An idea is born, a vision begins…

In May 2002, I bought a third share of the practice after again convincing a bank manager that I was worth my word and promise, though without assets or savings to back me up. It wasn't easy, but persistence and confidence made the impossible possible.

In that same month, the new era of laser dentistry arrived in the Southern Hemisphere. I was already sold on it and was the first to sign a contract on the new equipment. It would cost more than the practice I had just purchased - and wasn't to arrive until July.

I knew no bank manager would give me more money, as I was already heavily in debt and a very high risk. So, I turned to my mother and asked her to allow me to further mortgage her house to get the money. Too risky? Yes, no doubt about it. Yet, she agreed with total and unconditional belief in my crazy ideas and determination to make them a reality.

Soon after, I began going to the USA every year for advanced Laser training, joining an amazing group of colleagues who founded the World Congress of Minimally Invasive Dentistry. The group advocated a philosophy that totally harmonized with my views on providing dental services using highly advanced technologies, lasers and Microscopes, plus digital and environmentally friendly techniques that resulted in minimally invasive treatment.

And above all, dentistry that was health and prevention focused rather than knee-jerk reactive healthcare.

I quickly became the youngest Fellow, then Diplomat and Lifetime member of the organization, and was subsequently invited to serve on the Directors Board.

Did any of this happen just because I was there and seemed like a nice guy? Or did I earn it through hard work, diligence, and a belief in my own worth, while utilizing all my abilities in the shortest amount of time possible?

Lesson #6: Decision, dedication, and action are what got me noticed and rewarded for anything I have achieved. You can replace the "I" with "you" or the name of any person you know that has achieved success in life, relationships, wealth and health. That's the way it works - period.

Commitment

I started teaching and sharing my knowledge and experiences with my New Zealand colleagues in 2002. I was now 25 years old. It was humbling to be the first multiple laser dentist and educator in the country, but also it was a huge responsibility that I had decided to take upon myself. Further work was needed.

I began forming alliances with companies, institutes, and Universities wherever I could to further my education and open up new possibilities for me to teach. I spent more than I earned traveling, learning, and teaching. I was rarely paid in those first few years to educate.

During my efforts, I found a great mentor in Prof. Laurie Walsh, Dean of the Dental school in Queensland University and the ultimate authority in the field of lasers and high tech dentistry in the region. I attended most of his presentations in Australia outside of the university and one day, he made a point of asking who I was. I had been traveling to Australia repeatedly to learn from him and get my place in this field right where I wanted it to be: front row, first seat.

In 2004, I was invited to present with him in Sydney, and then Gold Coast, and the rest is history. I went on to present regularly alongside Prof. Walsh and other esteemed educators at large laser conferences in the region and all around the globe, by invitation.

Again, the law of attraction applied to get me where I wanted to be and with whom I wanted to be.

During this same period, in 2003, I decided to start my own educational and professional development institute. There wasn't a single private Advanced Dental/Medical Education Institute in the country at the time. I didn't know how or exactly when, but it was crystal clear in my mind that I would do it.

I also wanted to re-invent and evolve the way dentistry was done, involving the whole personal experience of the people coming in to seek our services. So, I decided to create a high tech dental spa and an educational Institute in one.

No one in New Zealand had heard of that combination before and I was considered a lunatic to even talk about it, especially at my young age and high debt level. My wife and my business coach, David, were the only people I could talk to about this idea. I had their full support and I needed valor to carry on realizing this dream.

Now that the vision is sorted, there is the need to figure out HOW?

4D...

Now

I will talk about different parts of the creation, evolution, tribulations, and ultimate success of the Laser lifeCARE Institute in the next chapters to show the application of my 4D's of success.

As we stand today in 2012, it is my humbling joy to state that the Laser lifeCARE Institute is a worldwide hit. By the written, video, and spoken testimonials of our international and local guests (that's what we call our patients) and of colleagues from the dental and medical specialties who have visited or trained with me at the Institute, we are leading a new generation of innovation and change in our profession, from design to technology and from guest-care (patient service) to education.

In 2005-2006, I had borrowed more than $1.2 million to build and set up the Institute, plus I had old debts that I had carried over from the prior practice and equipment, all at age 28. This meant that the apparent success and high turnover did not translate into personal financial gain until 5 years later.

In October 2010, a health corporate partner invested $1.8 million to co-own the Institute. This allowed me to take care of the huge debt I had held for the past 4 years. This partner is currently using many of my ideas, the Institute, and me as a model clinic to inspire others in their portfolio.

Most of the money I received from that $1.8 million fund investment was used to further upgrade our technology, pay off the business debts and the mortgage on my mother's house, purchase new cars for my sister and mother, and help my family and my wife's family enjoy better lives. I tithed a significant amount, as that is my duty.

The remaining money was invested in further personal development and mentorship and to finance my next projects. These projects had been dreams in my mind and research projects for a few years already. They include my own all-natural, alkaline and prebiotic oral/dental care products www.ozospa.com and the LaserKids Dental Clinic www.laserkidsdental.co.nz, which is the evolution of the Laser lifeCARE Institute to serve children and teenagers with our same technology and philosophy.

My loving family and I still live in a rented apartment in Auckland CBD. Money was never the goal; it was a tool and then a result of applying the 4D Leadership steps to success, which is a journey in time that continues...

THE 4D's

DR HISHAM'S 4D FORMULA FOR LEADERSHIP SUCCESS

$(D1 \times D2) + (D3 \times D4) = SUCCESS$

D^1 DREAM

D^2 DESIRE

D^3 DO

D^4 DETERMINATION

D1 = Dream

A dream is a vision, built upon a series of thoughts that transcend the realm of our physical world beyond all four dimensions, including time.

Thoughts are not bound to any kind of limitations, even those that bind energy, so we are able to dream of any thing, any time, and in any state, conscious or subconscious.

Whether our dreams make any sense or not is irrelevant at this point in the process of creating success. The relevancy is the fact that dreams transcend time and space. They are our way of tapping into the divine power of the Universe; and therefore, we can be at all places at the same time, in our dream.

Dreaming is a unique gift given to human beings by the Creator. No other form of creation can aspire to become, do or attain anything beyond their existing state of being. Animals dream during their sleep, but they do not dream while awake, of becoming more than they are. We can dream about anything we want through creative thinking.

We Live to Aspire.

While everything vibrates energy, that energy and frequency is preset and will never change until an external force of energy is applied to it. Examples include water becoming steam when heated or a stone crushed into powder with force or an animal reacting when placed under stress. Animals live to survive, we live to evolve and progress.

Human beings have the exclusive rights to change their state of being and energy vibration through thinking and dreaming. It allows us to create. Any human being, at any point in history and in all states of being, has the ability to dream and therefore create things, feelings and situations in their mind.

That is not to say these thoughts or dreams will materialize or won't. It is just a statement that this is the absolute potential we have, period.

Given that we have the potential to control our thoughts and dreams, it makes sense for us to make use of that potential to succeed or become leaders in our lives. For those aspiring to become, achieve, or attract more in their life, I can honestly say this is where it all begins, but not where it ends.

Every evolution of an idea, innovation, or new reality was once a dream in some person's mind. The simple truth is that everything starts with thoughts that become ideas that formalize into a dream. That applies to attracting the relationships that you want, to earning more money, leading a fulfilling life or inventing something and all the way to changing the world.

A dream is a mental vision
of what could be.

Logic has got nothing to do with all of this and neither does knowing how. A dream is a 'what could be' concept. The next chapters will discuss the 'why' and then the 'how' concepts that have to follow the 'what could be' in order for a dream to have the chance of becoming reality.

Awareness is what determines our level of dreams. If you are not aware of your potential, ability, current situation, or level of vibration, how can you dream of more? Each level of awareness leads to another step up in our level of dreams, creating more cognizance and opportunity.

I believe that humans have never invented anything in history. Rather, we discovered countless things through our increased awareness. Since everything is energy, that just is, and cannot be created nor destroyed, but can only change form, then our increased awareness and dreams of creating new realities have led us to discover ways to channel these already existing energy forms into new forms that give us function.

This may seem weird at first, but please think about it.

Was WiFi always available during the whole existence of the known Universe? Of course it was! So, why is it that its common use has only come into being in the last 10 years or so? Because somebody discovered a way to transfer data through existing radio waves (electromagnetic energy). I may not know exactly how that works, but I'm certainly grateful someone had that dream and then applied it.

Did the person who discovered transmitting and receiving radio waves more than a hundred years ago, Heinrich Hertz, imagine this use of those same cosmic energy waves? Definitely not.

The awareness at the time did not allow anyone to dream of such crazy things. It was crazy enough to make a box of wood speak on demand, by tuning into a frequency vibration!

There wasn't a need or use for WiFi at the time. We did not have "data" to transmit and receive. We did not have the Internet, computers, iPads or smartphones. The technological realities of today and the depth of their impact on our daily lives might have been a wild imagining in the beginnings of this tremendous discovery, but no one could yet dream of it.

Every one of today's technological "inventions" are in fact "discoveries" by the brilliant human mind of how to use and channel existing energy and materials to create something new, and then put it to effective function that matches with emotional needs. Then others come along to improve upon that discovery and make it better over time. This is representative of human evolution based on our innate aspiration for more.

Steve Jobs said it best in his quote, "Here's to the crazy ones... they push the human race forward, and while some may see them as the crazy ones, we see genius, because the ones who are crazy enough to think that they can change the world, are the ones who do."

"Invention and discovery happen when somebody has a dream to add value to the world by channelling existing energy sources to better use. Simple, but it's never easy."

Dr Hisham Abdalla

When it comes to applying these concepts of creating new realities in your daily life to accomplish whatever it is that you may aspire to achieve, the way to begin is to dream the outcome.

Success in life means <u>realizing</u> what you <u>think about</u> achieving - so think it.

Then, organize those thoughts into a dream and write it down. Keep dreaming that dream, until you achieve it or you feel that it no longer serves you.

It might seem that I am stating the obvious, but I am declaring that this is and has been something I learned, and then I just applied it. Now I'm telling you how it works. I believe it is the essence of any spiritual, motivational, or leadership teaching, yet many people are not aware of it or of how to apply it.

If you want to be successful in life and to lead yourself, your family, your organization and others, to a better future, then I advise you to set your own level of dreams. Don't let circumstance, or what you perceive to be real, set them for you.

"Dreams control your destiny, so make it a conscious choice to dream that destiny. Otherwise, it will be done for you by circumstance. One choice makes you a Victor, the other a Victim. Yet either way, you made a choice."

Everyone that we consider successful, innovative and inspiring, who lives in abundance, had a bigger dream. It has to be that way as stated by the laws of the Universe. Do you think Steve Jobs had little dreams and that he just worked hard trying to get somewhere - wherever that was? That is simply illogical, considering what Apple represents today.

To me, Apple is much more than one of the richest and most successful companies to ever exist - it represents big dreams of adding value to the world with irrational ideas of things that didn't yet exist, that were made real, desirable and admirable. The emotion, function, design, flow, integrity, and reliability of the whole dream are all translated into the individual products, systems, and company culture.

When the Rev. Martin Luther King said: "I have a dream. We must concentrate not merely on the negative expulsion of war, but the positive affirmation of peace. It is not enough to say we must not wage war. It is necessary to love peace and sacrifice for it" he was serious about sacrificing his life for his big dream to lead change in the world around him.

You see, we are all sacrificing our lives for dreams. Therefore, the questions before us are:

1. Whose dreams are they - truthfully?
2. How big are these dreams?
3. How much value do these dreams add to my life?
4. How much value do these dreams add to the world around me?

I know that a big dream makes you unstoppable. Big dreams do not create ripple waves, they create tidal waves. You are going to live your life anyway, so you may as well dream big. That's because, big or small, it takes the same amount of effort and time to dream. It's really not costing you more, so make it a BIG dream.

I believe Nelson Mandela when he said, "There is no passion to be found in playing small, in settling for a life that is less than the one you're capable of living".

Big dreams lead to big success. Leadership starts with big visions. Nobody wants to follow somebody with small vision or no vision at all. If you want to succeed and lead, you have to dream it big and visualize an ideal to work towards.

Consider that ideals are not always meant to be met, but to serve rather as targets to work towards. If you don't reach the ideal, but come really close, you can at least know that you've made headway. There is no other way to advance the human race except by making progress gradually while aiming towards ideals.

"We do not live in a perfect world, so do not fear perfection nor idolize it, for it is an illusion."

Just aim towards your ideal and celebrate excellence once you fulfill it as your new reality. Earl Nightingale said it short and sweet, "Success is the progressive realization of a worthy ideal".

My first rule of happiness is being grateful for everything that I have. Some people may find this conflicting. How can you be grateful and satisfied, but dream for more?

I don't see it as a conflict at all. Be grateful for what you have, be happy with who you are, but don't be satisfied. Dissatisfaction is the beginning of the creative state as it leads to bigger dreams. Enjoy today, tomorrow, and the whole journey being grateful, while in pursuit of being and having more. We live in an abundant Universe, so there is no need to be deprived or to be satisfied with deprivation.

My second rule of happiness is to be in harmony with my dreams and thoughts. Therefore, my dreams should be constructive, positive dreams of adding value to my life and the lives of those around me in hopes of creating progressive change. Attaining that dream earns rewards. These rewards may be emotional, physical, financial, materialistic, or all of the above.

Negative dreams create negative emotions and results that destroy. Thoughts of causing harm, war, revenge, stealing, or any other deleterious outcomes should be avoided at all times. Even if a dream involves you winning or gaining something big by going through such devious methods, please remember that what goes around comes around.

A big dream should consume you, so what do you want to be consumed by?

Since life is a journey and success is a journey too, there is no limit to the size or number of dreams you can have. There is no allocation system for dreams in the universe, so help yourself and keep dreaming.

Your dreams may change as your life progresses. That is totally normal and in fact important, because as your awareness and results change, you may change your mind about future dreams and goals. Keep adjusting your course and dreams, as you deem necessary, but don't give up too quickly on a dream that hasn't had time to be realized – not until you have exhausted my 4D's.

One of my biggest dreams that I am realizing currently is expressed in the Laser lifeCARE Institute www.lasersmile.co.nz and its associated value to my life and to the world around me since its conception in 2006. The dream was recently transformed in October 2011 by the opening of a second part of the Institute that serves children, the LaserKidsDental www.laserkidsdental.co.nz.

I envision a world full of happy, healthy people living in collaboration. I see people empowered with health awareness, properly applied knowledge and enduring experiences.

Peaceful and prosperous societies only come about through education, passion and sharing inspiration. That is what I dream of contributing towards.

With a vision of helping people "Look better, feel better and be better" physically, emotionally and mentally through my core philosophy: "Let's seek health rather than fight disease", I set out to formalize my dream. I dreamed of an Institute focused on continuous growth and development from within and extending out. I visualized a dental spa that emotionally impacts the senses of those who visit seeking help, advice, treatment, or enhancement. A place where an individual would feel appreciated and served, rather than treated as an ailment bearer. A place that utilized the latest technology and continued to evolve as technology advanced.

I wanted this Institute to be a beacon of inspiration and a driver for transforming my profession into the future. I wanted to share it all with the world. I declined to play the game of competition, which comes from thinking lack and limitation. I would rather collaborate in abundance with my colleagues and other fellow healthcare professionals of all specialties, to communicate a superior message that will benefit every human being whom we serve.

The Institute was to be a cradle for generating leaders at every level of the profession. Not just business leaders, but personal leaders committed to excellence. Excellence would be a habit, a paradigm that guided our consistency. Institute personnel would be hired for attitude and trained in new skills. This might not be easy, but with a big dream, very possible.

> I dreamed of creating harmony. Harmony is when individuals and their environment come together in concord to create a pleasing whole.

So, the place had to have a very specific architectural design flow that blended beauty with form and function. The logo was to be a piece of art prompting contemplations of what this place could be about.

The sense of sight was the first to be managed. The sense of smell managed next by using imported soy candles with a blend of bergamot and sandalwood. No one would ever be clenched by the typical look, feel, and horrid smell of a dental clinic when they walked into the Laser lifeCARE Institute.

The sense of taste was to be soothed by offering refined minted water, barista coffee, and a range of herbal teas and nectars. The sense of hearing stimulated with varying tones of music to suit many tastes and take people through little journeys of excitement and relaxation – not one boring monotonous style or just a radio playing. Then, the sense of touch was thought through. I wanted people to touch things that felt clean, fine, and cozy. I imagined a relaxation suite where people would chill out on a chaise longue in spa robes and fluffy slippers while waiting to be served.

You see, I knew my dream facts and then I set out to change the reality surrounding them. The fact is, dental treatment is never going to be fun to receive, no matter what cool technology is used. What I set about to do was to make it minimally invasive, as painless as possible, and to offer relaxing sedation options.

Above all, I set out to create an experience that outlasts the procedure, in the person's memory.

People forget many things, thankfully, but they will always remember how we made them feel. That flash of memory happens as soon as we cross their mind or path again. Create an outstanding experience of service, if you want to succeed in any people-serving business, which are all businesses really.

I did not intend to provide reactive dentistry, so there was not to be a Yellow pages ad or a sandwich board on the street. People would have to find us through existing guest's referrals, through our website and online presence, from magazine articles and TV appearances, or through referrals from other doctors, dentists, and specialists. People have to hear a story about us or research our story for themselves before they come to see us. That was how I intended it to be.

I had a vision of a new vocabulary that would elevate our verbal expression of our service. So, I changed the lingo of my profession. We do not have patients or clients, as some dentists call their patients, we serve guests. We appreciate people and treat them as guests, as if they were coming to our home. They are not all coming to us in pain and disease, so why should they be labeled with a name that indicates that? We use the guest's first name as much as possible, except if they prefer to be called by their surname. I am Dr. Hisham, not Dr. Abdalla, and many times just Hisham.

Guests deserve a friendly approach. A concierge greets guests in a lounge, rather than a receptionist behind a counter in a waiting room. The words express different meanings, but the role and actions of the concierge are different to a receptionist also. A Concierge is there to serve, not to check in and out. So, we serve, shake hands, welcome people in, show them around, make them a drink, and ask them to make themselves comfortable - not to take a seat. Concierge arranges accommodation and pick-ups for guests from out of town. Corporate cabs are arranged for guests who need a ride back home or to work and parking assistance is provided around the beautiful park across from our front door.

The guests are seen in a consultation room first, after unwinding in the relaxation suite. Treatment and financial plans are discussed in the privacy of the consultation room, with the full digital photography and radiography disclosure displayed to the guest on an iMac screen. When people can see everything and ask questions, they become involved. They start co-diagnosing and making their own decisions. That's in contrast to commonly being intimidated by the dentist's plans for them while they are helpless and scared under the dental chair light. Once each guest's consultation is complete, they are escorted to the dental suites for actual treatment, examination, or final diagnosis.

The people who serve in the Institute are never to be called 'staff' for that sounds too much like 'stuff'. They are a team, and I am one of them. Team members serve each other and serve the common goal of winning the game. Every role is critical and every team member matters.

We wouldn't have dental assistants, as do other dental clinics. We would have GuestCare nurses. There would be no front desk person, a practice manager or other similar positions and terms used within the industry. We would have a concierge, teams and team leaders, and project managers. New terminology had to be crafted to suit my dream. Nothing was accepted as conventional or as it has always been. I was creating a whole new world within my profession, for my dream to become reality.

At this time, I will not continue explaining how advanced digital technology and lasers help make dentistry a pleasure rather than a pain. That is the subject for another book. Suffice to say they provide great outcomes, unlike anything being done conventionally.

The philosophy dictates the technology, not the other way round.

The Professional Development Center within the Laser lifeCARE Institute is a state of the art educational facility. Live video feed from my surgical microscope and HD video cameras to the conference room create a truly interactive environment to share our and other innovations, technologies, and modern philosophies of treatment. We apply the same level of service and enduring experience to those professional colleagues who come for learning as we do for our guests. Quality catering, barista coffee, herbal teas and nourishing snacks are the standard of care, plus more. They are our guests too. Everybody who walks into the Institute is my guest.

It is easy to talk about all of this now, six years into the reality of my dreams. At this point, I am simply stating facts that I live through every day and the testimonials of the many people who have come to visit, learn, or be treated at the Laser lifeCARE Institute from around the globe confirm those facts. Everyone has an inspiring 'wow' experience.

While others now embrace my dream's reality, imagine how hard it was at the beginning of my dream, over seven years ago, to persuade anyone what my dream looked like before anything was real? When there was nothing like it, nothing to compare it to?

Between 2003 and 2005, I wrote down the thoughts and ideas that formed the parts of my dream and pursued my course. Yet, during that time, whenever I shared more details of my dream, I was laughed at, ignored or considered a total madcap. Some said it couldn't be done, some said it wasn't needed, some said it might work, but they didn't want any part of it as it was too controversial and risky. Some said that it could work if I changed this or that or the other to a more "normal" variable. Only a few people could share my vision and encourage me to continue.

In 2004, a respected colleague from Maryland stated, "I want stock in you Hisham, whatever that dream is, you're gonna make it happen".

We all need others to believe in us and support us during our journey to success. Find those few who will and leverage your ideas and dreams through their encouragement. Avoid the masses that tell you all the reasons why your dream is foolish and advise you to "get real". The only part they may be right about is that most great ideas and dreams never see the light of reality. But that isn't because they were worthless dreams; rather it is because nothing was done about them.

Dreams do not materialize by themselves.

That is exactly how it all started for me, without knowing how I would make my dream real – my seemingly irrational big dream that was born in my mind and fired my heart.

And eventually, by applying the rest of the 4D's, I built it into reality.

Come along - and read on…

CHAPTER 1 NOTES

"Dreams never come true by wishing, even in fairytales. Dreams only come true when passionately desired in the heart and acted upon, with a definite determination to succeed."

Dr. Hisham 2011

CHAPTER 2

D2 = Desire

Desire is the passion in the heart and the fire in the soul that drives a person to move towards their object of yearning. Desire to achieve a dream is the next dimension in the game of life, success, and leadership. It follows from a conscious decision to commit to your dream and vision, which then starts a subconscious transformation that creates emotions and belief.

That is the second dimension: D2.

D2 is a true heart's desire, not just a wishful thought about a dream or a good idea that may seem nice to have or achieve. A clear decision to commit ignites a fire of passion to go after your heart's desire.

There is a great difference in intensity between dreams and true heart desires. We speak of broken and mended hearts, good and bad hearts, brave hearts and fire in the heart. We know that the heart is the center of emotion. And without emotional drive, without heart, there is no way you can achieve your dreams or attract success in your life. Attempting leadership without strong desires and emotions is like trying to drive a car without an engine. Despite your intention and vision of where you want to go, you are not going to get anywhere.

The Divine energy that permeates the Universe responds to thoughts tied to strong emotions, not wishful thinking.

Until you hold a strong mental image of your dream and a strong desire to achieve it in your heart, you do not really believe in it nor do you really expect to get it. That is how the formula works.

To expect, you have to believe, and when you expect, you may receive.

Some things may be received from the Universe by the affirmative repetition of the emotional attraction of your dream. Serious success in life involves a bit more than that, but it begins here. This is where you start to attract the courage, energy, skills, people, and resources needed to continue your journey.

This is where you start to crystallize the 'why', now that you have established the 'what' through the D1: Dream dimension.

"It's the repetition of affirmations that leads to belief. And once that belief becomes a deep conviction, things begin to happen. Champions are made from something they have deep inside them - a desire, a dream, a vision."

Muhammad Ali

'Why' is an emotional question. If you find enough internal reasons to go after your dream without hesitation or distraction, you will shorten your journey through the fourth dimension of time. Why we do whatever we do is because of our emotional desires to gain pleasure and avoid pain.

My understanding of human internal motivation is summarized in these two core emotional drivers: pain and pleasure. Notice that I said emotional pain and emotional pleasure, not physical or mental.

Everything we do in life and how we behave is based on our subconscious mind associating actions and results with emotions. Feelings are emotive states of vibration that we align with our core values and beliefs. These sets of values and beliefs, which we develop over our lifetime, set the parameters of our subconscious mind. They give it the 'ruler' by which to measure whether an idea, a situation, an incident or a person will fit into our paradigm box or not. This ruler measures our feelings, i.e. emotional reaction, as pain or pleasure elicited by that certain interaction.

This explains why people behave differently in the same situation, given the same challenge and experience. It's their subconscious emotional rulers that are different, not the reality of the situation. Therefore the reaction may differ dramatically, or be the same. A situation that upsets someone might elate another. Some people believe that they deserve to be happy and prosperous and some don't. Therefore we cannot simply bundle all feelings and emotions into either a good or bad basket. What makes the difference is whether a specific feeling elicited by thought or action translates into a Pleasure Emotion or a Pain Emotion within an individual's mind.

> Everything we do is exclusively driven by our basic drive to attain pleasure and/or to avoid pain. Nothing more and nothing less motivates us.

Let's put this in perspective.

If I associate loving my wife or child with emotional pleasure, then I will do more to expand that love in order for me to feel more of that emotional pleasure. If I associate love with emotional pain due to past experiences or programmed core values, then I will do whatever

I can, subconsciously, to avoid love. Some people harm others in the name of love. That is obviously not a good application of love, but it is the emotion they are programmed subconsciously to associate with love, that is actually the problem.

Therefore, love, as a feeling, cannot be categorized as pleasure or pain, good or bad, positive or negative. It is only when a person's programmed core value (paradigm) is applied to the situation at hand that either pain or pleasure emotions result and drive the actions that follow.

Hate is not good or bad either, what it is directed towards and the actions it evokes are what make good or bad. I hate ignorance and apathy and will do anything to avoid the emotional pain of being ignorant and apathetic. That is good hate – for me – because it drives me to learn and act more to avoid emotional pain.

Hate of other people, for any reason, which leads to wars, crimes and discrimination, is a very negative application of hate. It drives such individuals to eliminate the apparent source of their emotional pain, those 'others', while totally ignoring the fact that it is their own core values associated with that hate that are the real problem. Right here you can see two distinct applications of hate, with two contrasting outcomes, just because of our own paradigms setting the stage for our actions based on the hate/love that we feel.

Some individuals associate abusing their kids, animals or other people with emotional pleasure. It may give them a false sense of supremacy or power or whatever. We all know that is wrong to do, but the fact remains. Until that driving emotion of pleasure is changed in that person's subconscious mind to an emotion of pain associated with the expressed behavior, the activity would continue. Some people enjoy physical pain as it brings them emotional pleasure. While others, like me, have little tolerance to physical pain as it brings them emotional pain which is much more intolerable than the physical pain itself.

Applying the core emotional drivers of human behavior to our subject, leadership and success, is something one must understand and master over time.

Your desire and dream can only drive you if they are associated with attaining emotional pleasure. If they do not harmonize with your paradigms (habitual ways of thinking or core values) then the opposite will happen. That same noble desire and great dream will now cause you emotional pain. This means that no matter how much your conscious thoughts say: yes - go forward, your subconscious mind will say: NO, STOP RIGHT NOW, PAIN AHEAD.

This is the process of mental sabotage. This is the reason many people cannot give up addictive behavior even though they know very well that it is physically harming them and many actually want to stop, consciously. The subconscious mind will always dominate in our lives and its programming is our code.

The good news is that you can reprogram your subconscious mind and change your core values and paradigms. It takes time and dedication using different techniques. It is beyond the scope of this book to recommend or discuss any method in detail. Some generally accepted methods include prayer, meditation, hypnosis, Neuro-linguistic Programming NLP, EFT, affirmations and more. Find out about which ones suit you and elect where and how you want to use them.

My point is that you have to be aware of how your current dreams and desires relate to your ingrained paradigms. That enables you to recognize whether they align or not and what to do about it. If the dream and desire are big enough and they collide with your paradigms, you will suffer immense emotional pain.

One of the two will have to change, either the dream or your paradigm. That is a choice only you can make and the responsibility is all on you.

Usually a true heart's desire will be in harmony with your paradigms, for the simple reason that you cannot sincerely desire that which is impossible for you to achieve. Dreams can be different, beyond belief and reality, but true heart desires take more than a flash to develop.

That makes them closer to the truth of what could be. It sounds strange, but it is as if it's been designed this way.

––––––––––––––––––––

Of pertinent note is the need to learn how to apply this understanding of the two core emotional drivers to influence others. If you want your spouse, partner, family or kids to love you more, find their emotional triggers. Then behave in certain ways, doing and saying things that entice them to feel more of that emotional pleasure and steer away from pain. They will feel really good to be around you, because your behavior reinforces their emotional pleasure. The same applies to your work colleagues, bosses or employees, your customers and the people you serve.

The more methods, techniques, and tools you can uncover and implement to facilitate people feeling better around you, the more you will be desirable, successful, rewarded, and worthy of leadership. The people who are not in harmony with your intentions and desires will either not be attracted to you and your business or they would leave your sphere of influence. This doesn't make them worse or better than you, just people with other paradigms, values and desires.

This is important especially in business. Your purpose should never be to serve and please everybody, because that is impossible. So, don't worry about the ones who leave, as long as you know that you haven't done anything wrong that needs to be amended. Focus on those you are attracting by doing everything right. Stick to your desired dream and principles and let the others find their own way in life.

Accept them, even when they make choices different to yours.

The Laser lifeCARE Institute was a tremendous learning experience relating to this concept. In the beginning, when things were tough and people didn't know about us, I worried about retaining every guest and trying to please everyone who came in. I would be upset for days when I learned that someone decided to go somewhere else. Eventually, I realized that I could not compromise on my principles and desire of providing the best level of care and service possible, and if someone's paradigms didn't match with what I was trying to provide, or simply didn't like us, then it was their choice to seek service elsewhere.

The interesting thing is that many have come back after months or years of absence to say essentially the same thing: "I see now what you were trying to tell me and offer me. I had terrible experiences elsewhere and now want to be here, where I will have the best experience". Their paradigms and awareness had changed, so their desire evolved. Time is a great revealer of truth. Some never changed their paradigms and I wish them all the best in life, with love. We have attracted numerous new guests from all over the globe who have come seeking services that are in harmony with their paradigms.

I guess this was my lesson in the law of attraction through desired intent from the Divine: keep doing what my heart's desire dictated to me, as I would have had done upon me, and then let go of the attachment to the outcome.

"Desire to be desired by treating others as you would like to be treated."

Let me tell you a little twist to all this. A true heart's desire should cause you emotional pain if you don't pursue it. Otherwise, you are still at dream stage.

What this means is that a big dream should bring you a sense of emotional pleasure when you hold its vision in your mind. A heart's desire burning with passion should cause you emotional pain that will drive you even harder to do something about it, to stop that ache from persisting.

Pain avoidance is a much stronger emotional driver than pleasure seeking.

In my experience, that desire to create and succeed had to build up and reach a certain threshold, until I just had to act on it or it was going to consume me. It became like the end of gestation period when the baby has to be delivered and nothing can stop it anymore. The subconscious mind started to fire on all cylinders so much so that it blundered my conscious thinking. All I could think about was how do I get all this done, when I have never done it before? Where can I find the money, people and resources? What do I need to do and who do I need to become to get it done?

The pleasant dreamtime was over, now it was delivery time or I was to suffer the insistent agony of my heart's desire until I wilted.

Time for action = D3 …

"Great ideas and dreams without passion don't become burning desires to achieve. They perish and never see greatness. Passion ignites the fire in the heart that makes the dream hurt in the gut, until it becomes reality. That's how greatness happens."

Dr. Hisham

CHAPTER 2 NOTES

D3 = Do

"Do" is a verb and cannot be a noun. It means to take action.

Too many great ideas, dreams, and desires wither because their owner failed to understand the importance of the D3 dimension and procrastinated for too long. Many self-help books and programs unfortunately propagate this phenomenon, focusing only on thoughts, dreams, written goals and affirmations, but without developing the critical awareness and responsibility of acting upon them.

Thoughts need action to shape them into physical form.

Thinking about the best car ever to be made and desiring it with all your heart for 20 years, will never, ever make that car come together in front of your eyes. It may attract people and situations into your life as opportunities to achieve that desired dream, but you have to realize that and act on those opportunities. You have to do things that will create that car of your dreams. Things like finding out how to best go about it, who can help or advise you, where do you get the materials, funds, and other necessities from, and so on. You have to find these things wherever they are right now and bring them into your realm.

Everything is abundant in the Universe, but energy never comes together into form until you actively take things from abstract to realism.

Paintings don't appear on canvas by focusing thoughts on the canvas and neither do fields get ploughed through dreams of the mind. Do things that will move you towards your target and the target will move towards you through all the four dimensions of the Universe, including space and time.

Do something now. Start with figuring out the "how"…

Until now, all you had to do was use your mental abilities to create thoughts and ideas, which became D1=Dream representing the 'What'. Then, you had to use your heart to develop emotional connections to your dream, which is D2=Desire representing the 'Why'.

Now, you have to engage the rest of you: brain, arms, legs, eyes, ears, tongue, and all. You have to take action, D3=Do, by learning about how to achieve your dream. Then, begin to actually make your dream a reality.

Procrastination is the leading killer of dreams. Its antidote is the action verb: DO.

The other side of this is people who work hard at doing a lot, all their life, while wondering why on earth they are not getting anywhere. Yet, when you ask them where they were supposed to be according to where they were going - they have no idea. They know it should be a better place than where they are now, but they aren't sure where that place is. Funny that.

Doing things in life randomly, without purpose and intent, is like driving your car around your whole life without a destination, until you run out of gas in the middle of nowhere. Drat, if only I had more gas, I would have got somewhere! Really, where?

That sums it all up so far. To get somewhere you have to think about where you want to go and why, decide that you will, figure out the way, and then - get up and go there. You must follow the sequence of the 3 D's as they're set up. You can't skip one or start at another if you want true fulfillment.

This sounds childishly simple; yet life seems so much more complex than that to most of us. I no longer think life is complex, but do think that life is not easy due to other people, circumstances, and ingrained paradigms that can hold us back or create diversions along our way.

So, life is not easy and sometimes not fair, as many would love to remind us, but I accept that fully. And because it is hard and I have to live it anyway, I want to struggle my own struggles, go my own way, make my own mistakes, learn my own lessons, and get to my own destination, despite the detours and bumps. I don't want to struggle and get to nowhere, or worse where someone else wants me to be for their benefit and my detriment.

I do not wish for life to be easier on me than it is on others, I just want to be ready and better equipped to deal with the dodge balls thrown at me while I am on the way to my 'top'. I need to do many doings, but mainly to learn, practice, apply, and share. All these important activities lead to better skills in tackling life. They are action-oriented deeds with vision and desire to back them up.

_____

Freedom to do comes with responsibility to act.

What I mean is that your actions should be in good faith, with good intentions, and aiming to achieve your higher levels of desire. Never do anything to harm or deceive others on your way to your dream. That will and should come back to punish you sooner or later. Religions and spiritual leaders throughout history have been telling us exactly that; virtue and responsibility for our chosen actions are part of the package, not an extra 'tick the box' option. If you do good, you shall be rewarded, and if you do bad, you shall be punished. The same emotional pain and pleasure drive is in action again, as discussed previously.

"You are obliged to accept responsibility for the consequences of your chosen actions. Otherwise, you cannot be free."

Personal freedom does not come from political systems or the lack of them. The only way one can be truly free is by controlling their own thoughts, desires and actions while accepting full responsibility for the outcomes they have manifested.

Until then, a person can never change their reality no matter what rights they may have or not have. If you don't like what you are getting, change what you have been doing. Move on and up and stop complaining about everybody else and everything around you.

Do take action to correct wrongs that you see, do make better whatever you come in contact with, and do add value through your actions.

One great leader and philosopher, by the name of Michael Jackson, said: "If you wanna make the world a better place, take a look at yourself and then make a change. I'm starting with the man in the mirror, I'm asking him to change his ways."

Nobody has or will ever achieve anything in life without effort and resistance. Your choice is to put out the effort to go up the ladder or take the effortless way down the ladder. Making your way up can only mean the decision to apply personal effort. The path to success in life and inviting others to follow you as a leader is through consistent, worthy action and responsibility.

Doing also allows you to test your dreams and desires and to correct your course towards that target. Until you start to take action, everything is in the ether and you can never know if it works or not.

Doing something that works toward getting you closer to your dream is important, but more important is learning from what you don't do right. Mistakes are bound to happen and wrong turns can be taken by oversight. No blame and no guilt should be held long term once these are identified and corrected. Making mistakes is normal, whereas repeating them is foolish. To be aware of all this, you have to do and act and then analyze the results of those actions before moving on to the next level of action.

To quickly cut through the fourth dimension of time, it is much easier to pay for knowledge and learn through other people's mistakes and achievements in your chosen field or dream. This can help you avoid making the same mistakes and can give you a new platform from which to continue your rise upwards from their last level of achievement. Doing everything from scratch, without mentors and/or coaches, is not advisable if you want to reach a big goal fast.

"Learn from others so you can leverage your time of doing better. Then, share your doing so others can do better."

Doing is participating with the Universe in making your desired dream a reality. Consistent participation leads to great results and success. Making the decision to only produce excellent results means that you have to unswervingly do things in an excellent manner.

A rule of happiness in life is to do what you love to do. If you are not living this rule, then you have two options: Learn to love what you do or change what you are doing.

Simple? Yes, and yet, so many people keep getting it wrong and live a life of complaining that their job/business/profession/relationship does not serve them and is choking them. Well, the truth is, you made a choice to live that life and to continue living it every day. No one forces you to go to work or be in the relationship you are in every day.

Make another choice now: learn to love your life or stop and start doing what you love. There is no other way to live a fulfilled life. We spend most of our adult lives working and serving people and the planet, so we better enjoy it if we are to expect any growth, excellence, or worthy reward.

When I started acting on my heart's desire to create the Laser lifeCARE Institute, everything was ambiguous. I had to start figuring out how could I do things and who could help me best. I spent many months researching, talking, learning, deep thinking, and writing notes in my journal. I declined to let all the naysayers and seemingly impossible obstacles stop me. A successful friend once told me that impossible can also be read I'm possible, if you choose to - and I did.

I had a lot of endeavors to do and the more action I took, the more people and circumstances I attracted into my new realm. It happened exactly as they say in the books about the laws of attraction - weird, but true. I was invited to a VIP breakfast with President Bill Clinton and our former Prime Minister of New Zealand, Jenny Shipley, in Auckland in February 2006. Later that year, I had the privilege of having a VIP breakfast with Sir Richard Branson at the Hyatt Auckland. In between these fantastic contacts, there were many interactions with prominent business leaders, Rugby stars, and other celebrities. It wasn't the fact of meeting any of these astounding individuals that changed my life. It was the fact that I could and did that gave me reassurance to continue on my path of doing more to attract more, until I realized my dream.

I have strong memories of that time when I was working on figuring it all out.

I started looking for the right place in Auckland CBD, hiring the right designers and builders, and of course, finding the right team members. Getting the money to do all this was a whole separate drama. With my wife, I looked at many commercial buildings before finding the right one that was on the ground floor of a brand new building in an upcoming area of the CBD. It boasted ample parking and faced a beautiful green park. There was a great landlord as well.

The team at Gaze Commercial, whom we chose after many meetings, impeccably accomplished the design and build. We used them again in 2011 to create the LaserKids Dental. It was hard to describe to the lead designer exactly what I wanted and how it was supposed to look, but he got it. He actually drew it better than I had imagined it. The separation of the warm, relaxing elements from the cool clinical suites and then joining them in a functional flow with a very pleasing aesthetic outcome was definitely achieved. Harmony was created.

People and their environment must come together in harmony to achieve a pleasing outcome.

In 2005, when I signed the 10-year lease, developed the design and construction plans, and ordered the expensive equipment and I.T. outfit, I still did not have all the money! Totally irrational again, but I didn't let anyone with whom I was dealing see that I had any doubts. As the financial projections of starting all this on my own were not that great, even my trusted accountant said I should quit. So, I had to take other action.

I looked and finally found a colleague working in the CBD who agreed to join his practice with mine as an associate, enjoying the rise up from his little windowless practice. Based on two dentists starting immediately, the financial projections started to look better and lenders started to accept my idea, due to my persistence. I finally got what was needed, but that wasn't enough. The company who sold me the dental units agreed to make a one off exception and do an internal finance deal over 5 years on 12% interest. I agreed immediately and signed another contract.

Then, something interesting happened. The dentist, who signed the agreement with me to move his clinic when the Laser Institute opened on The 1st of April, stopped returning my calls. This was in March 2006, while construction of the Institute was in the finishing stages. I finally got a call from his receptionist saying that he could not go ahead with the deal and didn't know how to tell me about it face to face. So, now I had a worthless contract that had just helped me get more loans, but now it was all my risk. Everything was 100% dependent on my action and production to meet the demand of what was to come. I was disappointed that I had placed my faith and trust in this person, stressed out about what was to come financially, and confused about the reasons why this all happened at the last minute. All I could do was to forgive and let go, so I could move on.

I did just that and immediately attracted a wonderful colleague, Basil, who was excited to work with me part time in this new and unique place. He did not have his own practice yet, so there was no goodwill transfer which also meant we were pretty much starting from scratch.

I hired the best team members I could find to fill all the desired roles and spent a lot of time, money and effort coaching and training them. Three of my original team members are still with me today. I am still in contact with many of the other team members who left to live in other countries. That tells me now that I made great choices at that time.

People and what they do are the critical factors that make or break any business, culture or society. I kept repeating my philosophy and how I wanted it portrayed, reminding everybody of what Mother Teresa said: "Let no one ever come to you without leaving happier". Accomplishing that takes persistent action with the intent to sustain doing and serving in excellence.

On April 1, 2006, after years of dreaming, desiring, and doing, the doors opened and we let the world into the Laser lifeCARE Institute. My brainchild was born and now it was time to nurture it, keep doing, and let it grow...

Marta, my wife and general manager of the Institute, said during team training:

"Do I want to succeed or do I want to be comfortable? Success means stepping out of your comfort zone and doing more."

Marta Abdalla 2011

DO IT NOW

"Nobody knows the future, but you know it's coming. Let's plan for it rather than let it happen to us. We can't go back to the past. Let's just learn from its successes and failures, joy and pain, and then let it be. Let's live and act now.
The present is all we have control over. Let's do things better, now."

Dr. Hisham 2012

CHAPTER 3 NOTES

_____

D4 = Determination

_____

Determination is the character trait that separates the average from the great.

Determination is persistence in doing, applying, desiring, and dreaming what you have set out to accomplish despite all the hurdles, detours, and momentary failures along the way. Determination makes you get up when you fall down – and you will fall down – unless you never get up in the first place.

Determination motivates you to lead yourself and motivates people to be led by you. Nobody in the world cares about what your dreams and desires are and all the busy action that you are doing may well go unnoticed. If you let the whole house crumble at the first or second hurdle, people will forget you even faster.

The true mark of a leader that stimulates admiration from the audience (including your own reflection in the mirror) is the determination to keep building your house of dreams, rain or sunshine, until it is finished. Then, to keep enhancing it and making it better and better, for there is no best. That quality alone, over time, shows the world that you are a leader worthy of emulating.

Consistently applying your belief in your actions and desired dream attracts more harmonious vibrations from the Universe in the form of people who want to help you, work with you, for you, and to serve you. It manifests as more material and spiritual resources that fuel your growth and also the ultimate goal of material, financial and spiritual rewards.

Nobody gets wealthy or becomes successful by having a great idea that they fall in love with, do a few quick things to make it happen, and then stop. Nobody develops a lasting and gratifying relationship with another by falling in love, doing good once or twice to impress and 'get' the other person, and then stop. Don't take things for granted. Nobody enthused other human beings to be a force of change in their company, society, nation or the world, by just putting up a few slogans, doing a few nice things in a short period of time, and then moving on to play golf.

You get the point, right?

"To win is to be set and prepared to play the game, and then staying until the absolute end. There is no shortcut."

Out of all the 4D's of success, this is the one that bends the dimension of time towards your result. The first 3D's are critical and must be applied first, but without this one, D4, time will not bend to serve you if you did not serve your time.

Steve Jobs hit a home run when he said: "I'm convinced that about half of what separates the successful entrepreneurs from the non-successful ones is pure perseverance." That applies to every kind of success in life, not just entrepreneurial success. Business leadership is just part of life leadership.

Leaders must have long-term vision and perspective. A determined mind, constantly applying excellence at every step of achieving that vision, will get the most rewards.

Consistency and excellence in application give confidence to the persons working on the vision and others who are served by it.

People want to belong and be served by others who they connect with through trust. People need to feel confident they are part of a worthy vision. Changing the vision, and the core values of what you are doing, will confuse people and destroy their confidence and trust.

Determination drives discipline. The discipline to keep doing what you need to do and avoid doing what you need to avoid, evolves consistency that is reassuring. Discipline is a personal choice or can be imposed. The more discipline that you choose to apply in your daily life and your sphere of influence, the more consistent your results will become.

Consistency creates peace of mind for the leader, the team, and the people whom they serve. Everyone in the team has the good of the organization or society at heart. They do well what they know to do, while trusting that the others are doing the same. The people seeking service will trust that the consistency and determination will always serve them well. Consistency reduces stress and increases confidence in the outcomes and conviction in the dream.

Consistency evolves care. Consistently taking note of one's actions and results, plus notes of the service they are rendering and the impact it has on others, generates personal responsibility and pride in achieving and giving. Determination in being consistent for the greater good indicates that you care and people want to be cared for.

Just as the heart's desire may cause emotional pain if not achieved, determination may be an emotional pain, too. It can be a pain to keep serving the pleasure of doing what you love to do if the results don't show up immediately. It may feel like it's too hard to keep going sometimes, if the hurdles are getting bigger and the doing seems futile.

It's like driving a long distance to get somewhere where you want to be.

You have to have a reason, a dream, and a desire of where and why you want to get there. You have to plan your journey, and then take action to drive there. But that doesn't mean you're there yet! Time will pass, until you either get there, or not, depending on your determination to keep driving. You have to keep focused while driving in the right direction, taking calculated risks and getting back on track after detours that will happen along the way.

We all have a mental GPS (Global Positioning System) that we can set and reset to our desired destination. It may have some glitches and it may have to recalculate the route after unexpected detours on the journey, but the destination is set and will not change until we get there. The only way to not get there is to turn the GPS off and get lost or to change the destination all together. You may reset the GPS or simply ignore the instructions of your own GPS and go driving off in the wrong direction. None of this can be blamed on anyone else other than the owner of the GPS: you.

Your decisions always rule.

———————————

To imagine that there is any achievement without risk is like imagining life without death. One is part of the other. If you walk out on the street you are taking the risk of not getting back home, because many things can possibly happen. What do you do? Stay "safe" and don't go anywhere, do anything, or become anything? Or do you manage your risks by learning and understanding how to get to your destination, while avoiding most of the apparent risks?

Managing risk does not mean that the risk is gone, it just reduces the probability of that risk occurring and if it does occur, it reduces its impact. Not managing the risks means a higher chance of things going wrong and when they do, it can be catastrophic. Either way, risks must always be taken to live, let alone thrive in this world.

Be determined to take calculated risks, always be a learner and observer of what is going on around you. Be prepared to change course, not destination, if situations dictate so. Be ready to accept criticism and negativity from people around you. Take the fact that they are noticing you doing something different and better as a contribution to your drive to keep going. Make sure that your ideal is a worthy one, even if some call you 'contentious'. Your goal is to get there, no matter how many times you fall and get up, and no matter who says what. Once you get there, everyone will know that you were right and you will have earned the rewards and recognition. If you don't get there, then they were right and you took unnecessary risks and wasted your time.

> Make sure that your determination is bound to a worthy ideal and that your actions only empower that drive to move towards your desired goal, of providing better value to your world.

Be determined to celebrate your successes along the way, at every checkpoint. If the dream is as big as it should be, you won't get there in a blink. As much as it is important to detect and correct the detours, it is just as important to detect and celebrate reaching milestones along the path to glory. If you don't get enough encouragement from your expedition, the going can only get tougher. Share the celebration and joy with those who matter in your life and journey. The ones who are in the vehicle with you and those who support you will all want to be part of the celebration.

"Don't wait until the ideal is achieved, for it may never be the same as you set it out to be and you may miss the glorious moments of rejoicing in your own success."

Be determined to develop a solution-oriented character.

Leaders develop solutions to problems many times before the problems become eminent. Problem solving is important, but it is reactive. Active solution orientation is more ideal.

What this means is that your actual value to the world should focus on actively solving problems for others, hopefully before they even occur, rather than dwelling on the problems. When unexpected problems happen along the way, look quickly for a solution. Stop blaming and looking for the reasons why and whodunit! Identify the problem, come up with the solution, and apply it. Then, learn from it and make sure you let those around you learn from it as well. The determination to be solution oriented will save you time and stress, and make you a leader rather than a moaner or dictator.

Be determined to make your persistence worthy and known by sharing the results with those who care.

As I mentioned before, people only perceive what they can see, hear, touch, or interact with. They don't care about your inner motivation and dreams; they react to your achievements and what those mean to them. Your determination to share the vision, the actions, the methods, and the benefits of the outcomes will cause you to be viewed as a leader, even if initially it seems like nobody cares.

Ask for help when you need it, because you can never be everything to everyone or even to your own dream. Recognize your strengths and delegate your weaknesses to people who can do better than you. Don't let your pride overshadow your abilities to fulfill all the roles needed to execute your dream.

People do care about inspiring stories of struggle, perseverance and success. That is the story of our lives as humankind and the only reason movies and fairytales exist and make billions of dollars yearly. They all tell the same story in different ways and we all want to be engaged. We pay lots of money and attention to continue being engaged. Make your determination to succeed engaging to others, because you need their help, their recognition, and their payment.

Here is where all this came into reality for me as the Laser lifeCARE Institute (LLCI) story continued.

Soon after opening, the excitement of getting to the first step of the dream, despite all the prior obstacles and my father's recent death, I had more drama to face.

There were many little things that needed to be finished in the fit out, as they didn't turn out exactly as the designer had planned them. That is normal in any big project like this, but it was just one extra factor that was annoying me during our daily work. The brand new computers and network had many problems from the first month. Being an all-digital Clinic and Institute, we relied on them totally to function. That was really frustrating and costly. Of course, I solved that problem later on by going to Apple iMac's everywhere, as I had at home. This took a couple of years to gradually achieve, as I couldn't immediately afford to change the expensive 'brand new' IT system in the first year!

We had costs that crept out of control, monthly payments, rent and salaries that were totally incongruent with our turnover. People didn't know that we existed yet, except for my few loyal guests who transferred with me to the new clinic. I had to continue paying rent on my old practice for another 9 months as my old partners did not allow me to sell my share of that practice when I got out.

The lack of money got so bad that I began borrowing more from friends, nearly every fortnight, to keep paying salaries and bills. I took out a substantial loan from a friend at 14% and maximized the drawings on my mother's mortgage. We moved from the beautiful townhouse in Mission Bay to a small apartment in the city to save on personal expenses. We lived on credit cards. It was not going well at all.

Lenders and suppliers started calling for their overdue payments and I started to avoid those calls, as I was not sure what to say. My manager at the time did her best to deal with all this, but eventually it got to her. She couldn't deal with the stress anymore and wanted to bail out before the ship went down, so she resigned.

Everyone could feel my stress and my health started to deteriorate. I lost 13 Kg in 6 months and was throwing up every morning after disturbed sleep every night. I do not drink alcohol or take drugs, so avoided turning to such delusions during this time of extreme strain. At this time, I was also diagnosed with gluten intolerance after 29 years of eating gluten.

I felt that I was letting everyone I loved down, my family, my supporters and my guests. I worried that the naysayers were right and I was wrong. I worried that we may lose everything including my mother's house, my reputation, and the trust they all had in me. I would rather die than let this happen.

I just didn't know how to fix it - yet.

Everybody had a piece of advice for me back then. Change the name to something with "dental" in it, put a flashing sign or a sandwich board outside saying that you do dentistry, put out pamphlets and special offers, go in the yellow pages, let go of some team members, and so on. But, none of this advice fell within my intentions. It contradicted with the very essence of my dream: to elevate the game and provide quality by attracting quality.

I embraced my dream and kept doing what I do best, providing great dentistry and making friends with the people who came in as our guests. I lectured more and avoided the things I didn't want to deal with, such as the finances.

The first two-day, intense, Live Laser training I presented at the LLCI was in July 2006.

It was exactly as I had envisioned it and was like no other training ever provided in Australasia. We had a full house, with 10 dentists from Australia and 3 from New Zealand. I still remember them all and they remember me, 6 years later. We have kept in contact and when I travel to Australia to lecture or to attend conferences, I make a point to visit them. They still speak of that amazing training experience, and of the learning and hospitality we shared with them. Their positive reactions are humbling and very satisfying to me. This element of the Institute just kept growing and getting better and better, but it wasn't enough to keep the dream funded.

Ultimately, my team started to notice my withdrawal and that began to affect the very core of their commitment to the vision.

When the creator and leader of the vision withdraws, the vision starts to die.

I had to pick myself up and get back in my own game.

David, my business coach, stopped charging me for his services at that time, but was there to help and support more often than he did before. He kept reminding me of the big WHY that had originally started the fire in my heart, that I had pulled it off this far, and the consequences of giving up vs. going forward. He reminded me of the 4D's that I had spoken and written about in my journal. He reminded me that I am bound by my own rules.

He was absolutely right. I had to stick to my own rules, continue the journey towards target, despite all the apparent obstacles and diversions that I was going through.

My best friend Jerry, who also lent me some money at the time, kept reminding me of all the successes that I had gained since my arrival in New Zealand, saying: "I'll remind you of all this misery, in case you forget, 5 years from now, when you'll be too busy traveling the world teaching what you've created and enjoying the success. It'll all be a distant memory then." I can now testify that he was absolutely right. But, I couldn't see that at the time.

Time is a great revealer of truth as they say.

So, when it came to the crunch in October 2006, six months after opening and struggling, I had to call it in. It was make or break time, no more resources for borrowing and no more hope in avoiding any payments, simply time to do or die.

During fateful times like these, you end up surprising yourself with what you can do to save your true heart's desire and your dream.

What I had said before, that a worthy dream is one that you are willing to give up your life fighting for, I meant to put into action now. I had to plan a whole new strategy and with the determination of following through till the end, I did what I had to do.

I called in all my financial partners, lenders, landlord, and CEO's of my main suppliers to my boardroom. My accountant and friend, Bart, was there to hold me responsible to my plan and for moral support. I told them the truth, gave them our financials and the exact steps of my plan forward. I apologized for avoiding any of them before and reassured them that it would never happen again.

Open communication is very important during all times, comfort or distress. Another lesson learned.

It was up to them to decide to pull the plug now and we all lose or they give me 6 months of reduced rent, repayments, and extended credit. I realized this would add to the overall financial burden in 6 months, as all these allowances will have to be paid back on top of the normal payments. But, I made it clear that I was not asking for any charity. This was part of a new plan to really grow the amazing creature that I had established: the Laser lifeCARE Institute.

Most of those present had questions for me, but eventually they all went silent in thought and consideration. Finally, one gentleman spoke up, John Miocevic, senior advisor at Medical Assurance Society. Cutting through the silence, he said, "I don't remember any rational reason why we actually gave you the money in the first place and now, here we are wondering rationally what to do next. We lent you the money because of you, because we believed in you and your courage, being such a young brash professional. We already took a huge risk and I want to give you the advantage of being courageous again. We all want you to succeed, but there will be conditions and deadlines to meet…"

With that, the whole table started talking towards a resolution. New agreements were drafted and we all shook hands.

More trust means more responsibility. I was ready, determined, and grateful.

The moral within the recounting of this time of difficulty is that people are always willing to help and bend their rules for a worthy cause.

If you have a big dream that is struggling and you are doing everything to save it and are determined beyond a shadow of a doubt to complete the journey, people will want to support you when they are engaged and inspired by your fortitude.

"Give people a reason to engage in your story, then watch as that engagement transforms your story."

And then, more good things happened.

National TV1 and a business review magazine aired and wrote stories about us and what we were trying to achieve for our guests and for dentistry. My good friend, Dr. Yvonne Vannoort, who has a very special story with me, introduced us to Kathleen McKellar, a consultant from DDS, Australia.

Kathleen had a huge impact on my life at the time. She was very experienced, having done consulting for decades in the dental and medical fields and had been coaching all over the USA and Australia. She was very impressed with my vision and the Institute from a design and flow perspective and praised the level of service we were providing. She loved my story and wanted to be part of it. I was so glad that I was still inspiring people enough that they were offering to help. But, I could not afford any consulting fees, though I needed the services.

My vision and the Institute were a new challenge Kathleen wanted to take on, no matter what. We agreed that instead of paying her half the fee upfront for her services, as is customary for her business, we would pay her half in one year and the rest over a period of 6-12 months. She knew that a vision and commitment like the one I had started couldn't die if it just had more structure and systems.

I needed structure and glue added to my team and organization.

Over the next few months, she helped the team members buy back the vision and core philosophy, reinforced the details of the New Guest Experience we were providing, and made them take more personal responsibility and initiative than I had been able to ask of them. She challenged them to be better and they were!

It amazed me how people in an organization or society could rise up to such unexpected levels when challenged and given clear structure and goals. They liked me and loved the vision of the LLCI, but I was obviously not a good manager.

Leaders and innovators do not necessarily make good managers. I definitely was not manager material at all.

Clear instructions from Kathleen came through: "You are a dreamer, visionary, and a great influencer and dentist. Stick to your strengths and don't muddle up in what you don't do well. Someone else has to manage this place and apply the systems to see your vision through to fruition. You need to be looked after and left to shine where you naturally shine. Someone with a heart and real determination should be managing this place, and I know who."

Kathleen surprised us when she picked Marta, my wife, as the perfect person to manage the LLCI. Marta had been at every single meeting with me since the idea stage. She had been involved in the design and construction, in hiring the team members, and in the everyday activities of the Institute. She had been living the struggles and suffering the same as I had. As a hospital nurse and trained beauty therapist, her plan was to run the spa after we got the dental clinic and professional development parts of the Institute up and running properly. She did not have any management training and felt that her English was not good enough at the time to deal with such a big role. Yet, Marta took only a minute to absorb the new orders before saying, "Yes, I will do it."

She didn't have to know how yet.

You see, here is the same moral again. Despite all the rational reasons why she couldn't be a good manager at the time (language barrier, lack of skills, other focus and out of her comfort zone), Marta had the guts to take up the challenge. She shared the determination and was sold into the dream and burning desire just as I was. She had a personal vested interest in making this happen no matter what, and that's what mattered. The rest was all details that just needed sorting.

"Skills can be learned where there is commitment and attitude. Skills without a heart are a waste."

She studied, learned, grew, made mistakes, and learned again, until she flourished into the best general manager that I could dream of having. Her determination was so inspiring that she attracted exactly the same sentiments. People just wanted to be around and help her. Kathleen was her mentor for over a year and David became her business coach rather than mine. Many individuals and organizations prefer to deal with her now. They know that with her, they get results.

There were other systems that Kathleen had us develop and implement, but the preceding four paragraphs are the core of what made the whole Institute spin up and fly in the proper direction.

This is the value of a mentor who understands your vision and takes your determination to succeed to full throttle, implementing systems that intersect the angles and branches of the organization and dream.

Re-organizing the team was a critical step that Kathleen made us take.

Only one person resigned and my dear friend and associate dentist, Basil, left to study further and specialize. No one was laid off, as they were already the right people, just not in the ideal roles for their abilities. Every aspect of the philosophy and dream was kept intact and the New Guest Experience that we promised to deliver was untouchable. It became deliberately and consistently deliverable by a team of focused individuals, working towards a common goal, under a dedicated manager and led by a vision that stimulated them to keep going.

Everything changed from within and was expressed from without as a result. People began referring other people, colleagues began referring guests to us for specific procedures, and the rest is history.

We had to keep the determination of never accepting 'good enough' as our outcome. Excellent and always becoming better is what we kept going for and keep going for every day.

A year and a half later, when I could prove to the world that my new plan had worked with the help of mentors, friends and trusting guests, I invited the same people from the financial institutions, bank, landlord, and supply company CEO's to share our success and thank them.

There was a very different tone at this boardroom meeting compared to the one before. Laughter and merriment prevailed from the moment of their arrival at the LLCI. I thanked them all for their trust twice over and handed out the new financials. We were still heavily in debt, but everything was being paid on time, all obligations were being met, turnover was 300% above the same period a year and a half earlier, and continuing to grow beyond all projections. My personal production was in the top 5% of dentists in the country and was by far the highest they had ever seen for a dentist in my age group (30 years). It was a confirmation of the true teamwork that had been created and the trust shown to that team from guests who had received the best quality of care and were happy to pay for that value.

D4 – Determination, paid off in time.

The rest was natural growth fueled by the persistent application of our new systems, focused commitment to excellence, and the evolvement into better technology, philosophy, and higher levels of service and care. That evolution will never stop.

I would like to bring Dr. Yvonne Vannoort back into the story now. A moral of paying it forward, without expectations of immediate compensation manifested here.

Yvonne was in a similar arrangement to my old practice. She was in a partnership with two other colleagues who did not share her vision and did not want to incorporate lasers and the digital dentistry aspects into their practice. She wasn't happy where she was, but wasn't sure what to do about it. It was comfortable for her, but not satisfying.

She worked with me on Friday mornings during our first three months after the LLCI opened and attended our trainings. She didn't treat many guests during that time and hardly made any money from this arrangement. She later told me she was there for the experience, inventiveness, and to support me.

Then, one day in July 2006, towards the end of our long working hours, she came in and asked to talk to me in private. We sat in the relaxation suite as I listened to what she had to say.

She said she wished to thank me for the opportunity and the inspiration that I had given her and that finally she had resolved to go her own way. With her husband Jacque, who is a lawyer, she would be opening her own dental clinic modeled on my concept but with her own flair. She was ready to make the sacrifices and face losses by leaving her partners and current practice. She went on to explain that she had dreamed of this many times, but could never see herself being courageous enough to do it, until she saw what I had done. Lastly, she asked if she could use some of the ideas from the Institute that she loved and if I would be there to help if she needed advice.

I was too humbled to know what to say immediately, other than congratulations for summoning her valor and that she was welcome to any of my ideas that she wanted to use in her new venture with Jacque. I warned her about what came after, the huge monetary burden, and that the real struggle really began after the dream seemed tangible, not just before. I asked if she was ready for that financial agony and reminded her that it was comfortable where she was in the old practice.

Her eyes shimmered as she answered. "The dream is too big now and the desire burns strong. I cannot ignore it and do nothing to fulfill it anymore. It doesn't matter how hard it is going to be. Now that I know it can be done, I want my dream too, thanks to you." We both cried.

A few months later, Sanctuary Dental and Law was born. Yvonne's shared vision, struggles, and successes continued along with mine, as did our friendship. As I had mentioned before, Yvonne was the one who introduced me to Kathleen and that was a game changer.

Then, in 2010, Yvonne made me meet (despite my initial resistance to do so) with the lovely people from Dental Corp. They are the health corporate partners that we joined with a few months later. Their investment in the business helped me get rid of all our debts and evolve the Institute further. Yvonne and I were the very first clinics that Dental Corp had approached in Auckland and two of only three in the whole country. My inclusion was because of Yvonne's introduction.

So, there is the moral of paying it forward by allowing your vision and determination to inspire those around you in a totally open, caring way.

"The determination to win should never be confused with competition to keep others out of the way. It should invigorate you and the people around you to all win together."

I did not expect anything from Yvonne and only reveled in her move towards her dream, but Yvonne repaid me with an open heart and generosity beyond thanks. We continue to be friends.

"Passion makes the salty sweat of action and hard work taste sweet. Action is what we do to serve our burning desire of a great dream. It fuels the determination to keep us going against all odds. Passionate determination separates the legends from the achievers."

Dr. Hisham 2007

CHAPTER 4 NOTES

The equation

(D1xD2) + (D3xD4) = SUCCESS

To put it all together so far, I have come up with this simple mathematical equation for personal leadership and success. The next chapters will discuss critical qualifying merits of the person/people applying this formula.

The heart's desire D2 is an emotional multiplier for the thoughts and ideas that make up the dream D1. The greater either of these two is, the higher the level of personal drive towards achieving that goal. There will be no manifestation of the dream though, without adding the next two D's.

In applying action D3 and doing what needs to be done to realize the dream, the size of the outcome depends on the size of the action multiplied by the level of commitment to see it through, the determination D4 to succeed.

Obviously, the total magnitude of the outcome or success is reliant on all the four D's being of as high a magnitude as possible. If any of them is weakened; the other multiplying factors will pick up the difference and invigorate the passion of the whole formula to still move towards an outcome.

Once you understand and master the 4D's, you would have earned the success that you deserve. Expect it and it will come in time.

Being the fourth dimension of the Universe,
and something that we cannot control,
let time take its time.

To summarize personal leadership to success in 11 points, I would say:

1. Make up your own dreams in life. Don't be a slave to circumstances or to other people's dreams. The bigger the dream, the bigger the drive.

2. Write down your goals and dreams in life. Categorize those in terms of importance to the value of your chosen path in life and the legend you want to leave behind. You may have a singular purpose in life, but your goals are the multiple steps necessary to achieve it.

3. Pick the dreams that top your list, the ones most in harmony with your core values and paradigms. It is very important to identify and connect with your own core values and paradigms first, and then you will be able to match the dreams to them. The one with the largest impact on your perceived value in life is the one to focus on first. Your other dreams can follow or happen along the way with the big one. When it's accomplished, make the next dream number 1 and work on that as top priority. Always work on number 1 dream on your list the most, until another dream takes that position.

4. Make a conscious decision to pursue that dream with an emotional heart's desire. Conscious affirmation of a goal over a period of time, if meaningful, will imprint that dream as reality within the subconscious mind. Once it is at that level, you have made an emotional connection with your goal that will self-motivate your whole being towards achieving it. You will know it. The feeling of a heart's desire is undeniable.

5. Take action immediately. Don't put it off and kill your desire. Your desire for growth and achieving more is a built-in system in humans. If you dull it and ignore it, it will consume you. Living in regret of missed opportunities and going through 'what could have been' during your last moments on earth is a waste of a lifetime. You only have one shot at life, make it count.

6. Start the doing by learning how to best go about achieving your dream. Don't necessarily give up everything that you are doing right now, unless you can. Begin, at the least, by figuring out the 'how' and studying the possibilities.

7. Begin building your dream when you know just enough to get going, do it now. There is no other time that you can control except the present, act now.

8. Be absolutely determined to keep going until you realize your dream. Keep reading your goal and dreaming your dream. Keep the fire in your heart burning with desire for the outcome and keep taking action steps that lead you there.

9. Ask for help from the right people, not just anyone with an opinion, as there are too many of those. The right kind of people will appear when the right kind of focus is applied to the dream. It's the law of attraction in action. The opportunity will come, but you have to notice it and grasp it.

10. Aim for ideal, celebrate excellence and make sure that you enjoy the journey. With all its joys, trials and tribulations, life is to be lived with meaning. Find your meaning and lead your own story to success.

11. Always be grateful. Everything is a blessing, even if it is in disguise.

CHAPTER 5 NOTES

"Make your Dream matter. Desire it and Do it with absolute Determination to win. Be ready to give up your life for it, because you are anyway".

Dr. Hisham

Character and Culture

Character is the distinctive set of qualities that make up an individual and define their behavioral pattern. Culture is a collective sum of expression of the characters within a group of individuals. Culture can be as small as within a family or a business organization or as big as a society, nation, or world.

Character

Character comes from within, the thoughts and beliefs that one holds in their mind make one's character.

James Allen said it well in his classic As a Man Thinketh: "As a man thinketh, so is he. A man is literally what he thinks, his character being the complete sum of all his thoughts. As a being of power, intelligence and love, and the lord of his own thought man holds the key. Man is made or unmade by himself."

Your character, based on your core values and thoughts, determines your paradigms and habits. A paradigm is a habitual way of thinking. That, in turn, determines your actions, which determine your outcomes. All this happens by choice, conscious or subconscious, not by default.

So, if you make your own character, then you can change your character. It is not a genetic code; it is first affected by our environment growing up and all the input of our parents and society. Later, it is affected by our thoughts and the thoughts that we allow to enter from our environment. To be a leader of your own destiny, family, organization or society, your character must be worthy of leading.

Worth is not as much about the strength of character as it is about the quality of character.

Many people throughout history have led through strong character, but many used it to afflict evil on the world. Because of their own misguided thoughts and beliefs (character), they used their strength and influence to guide weaker souls into wars, killing, and destruction. It still happens all over the world today. Absolute denigration of humankind, as the master with the strong character safely gains power. They always fall in the end, but many innocents would have lost their lives on the way.

That is not whom I choose to serve with my message. I choose to serve people like you, who possess characters of integrity, dignity, and respect for oneself and for others. The characters that leave true legends and influence others to lead better lives, the ones with a conviction to serve humanity and contribute to the world, while accepting the rewards that come from that service as their earned value in the world.

Quality character individuals evolve a purpose in life. They question themselves often: Am I living up to the best in me? What can I do better today than I did yesterday? What can I do to serve others now that will make a difference?

We're after the qualities that make your character amicable, approachable, adaptable, and influential. To influence and persuade yourself and others, develop a character that relays Aristotle's Ethos, Pathos, and Logos.

Ethos relates to the ethical appeal, that gives your character credibility. Ethos is the Greek word for "character" and the word "ethic" is derived from it. It is what you portray to the outer world by your actions and words.

Pathos relates to the emotional appeal of your character and vision. Inspiring your life and others around you, as a leader of success, must involve an emotional connection.

Logos relates to the appeal of logic and reason. What and why are you doing what you are doing and how that has changed or will change the outcomes, with clear objectives and examples, are what we aim for here. Logos is Greek for "word" and the English word "logic" is derived from logos.

The ideal characteristics or CHARACTER TRAITS of a leader include, but are not limited to:

1. **Vision**
   This is where it all starts. Leaders have long-term visions of what could be. They see the future and create it. They make things happen. Followers dwell on the past and present, focused on what has happened or is happening to them.

2. **Courage**
   Leaders have the courage to express their visions, act on their desires, and keep persisting until they achieve excellence. Napoleon Hill in his all-time classic, Think and Grow Rich, talks about this: "Most ideas are still-born, and need the breath of life injected into them through definite plans of immediate action." It takes courage to breathe life into your ideas and to take a risk with "definiteness of purpose", as Napoleon Hill calls it, if you aspire to ever achieve or lead a better life.

3. **Integrity**
   There is no way around this one. Until people feel and see your integrity, you can never be seen as a leader. Even your own mind will get confused, if your character is not devoted to integrity. It is not an option; you cannot simply do things with integrity sometimes, when convenient. It is fundamental that you do everything with integrity all the time.

4. **Commitment**
   As a leader, you would develop a character of absolute commitment to your cause, vision, self-worth, and the good of the people you serve. Commitment to finish what you start, to correct your mistakes, and to do better and better is a core character trait of a determined leader. Be that.

5. **Concentration**
   The ability to laser focus on one or a few goals and dreams until they materialize is indispensable for a leader to succeed. Distractions abound, negative thoughts and obstacles are inevitable and silly habits of pleasing our animal instincts can all attempt to run our lives. Focus and concentrate on your definite purpose and what you came here to do. Let all the other stuff roll like water off a stone and hold your ground.

6. **Responsibility**
   Most people try to blame or make excuses for the bad things that happen in life. Leaders take responsibility for what is happening and fix things when needed. It starts with personal accountability for your own actions, words and circumstances, and the impact they have on you and the people in your world. This grows into cultural and societal responsibility to mend what others may have manifested through reactive thinking and apathy. Responsibility also means celebrating your success and the success of others in your world, to place emotional focus on that and attract more of it. Never forget to celebrate good and excellence when they happen. Happiness comes with a responsibility to share.

7. **Resilience**

This is not toughness, but rather pliability. Being able to adapt and reform when situations change, without losing focus, is critical to being a true leader. Adapting to people's changing needs, the changing world, and the emotional rides we take through our journey in time requires flexibility that doesn't bow or fall prey to reactive behavior.

8. **Respect**

Respect for self, for others, and for all the creatures on this world is one of the most pleasing traits of a leader's character. It evolves from accepting the truth that everybody and everything is related. We would not destroy what we respect, kill whom we respect or hate what we respect. So develop a character of respect to nurture and flourish.
Develop a character that deserves earned respect.

9. **Enthusiasm**

A leader who is not enthusiastic about their cause, vision, and actions cannot arouse a following and a movement. Develop a character of enthusiasm and passion; influence the world around you with your energy. Always be enthusiastic, but control how much you output based on the audience. Apply just the right amount of enthusiasm in everyday life situations. Be tactful when you are dealing with other people, don't scare them and don't bore them. Immense enthusiasm can be just what is required in many situations to make an impact and influence others. Enthusiasm is the path to lead people who are not as driven and need more understanding or motivation.
Adjust to each situation, without compromising who you are from the inside.

10. **Courtesy**

Be courteous and generous with your time, words, and possessions. Giving is the first step towards receiving. Go the extra mile, without being asked. Do that for one person every day, forever. Don't worry about that person being thankful or not. If they are not, fantastic, you showed them how to be better.

The habit of courtesy and generosity fulfills the soul's need to share. The attraction of goodwill and compensation will come from the Universe, not just the people you serve.

11. **Excellence**
My beloved word. Always aim to portray excellent appearance, language, behavior, actions, and results. Pay attention to the big things as well as to the small details - it all matters. Remember that like life itself, excellence is a journey and not a destination. Keep raising your standards of excellence, without anybody else demanding it from you. That is how you inspire others to lead similar lives, by evolving excellence.

Today's excellent is tomorrow's mediocre. To lead, you must create new levels of excellence that inspire others. Commit to excellence in your character, without compromise.

Culture

If you want to work with or for people, marry someone, serve or live with people, and produce children who are all exactly like you, rest assured that is physically and spiritually impossible. Nobody is exactly the same as another, even twins.

If you only want to deal with people who are like you in most ways, as in appearance, race, culture, beliefs, spirituality, and intelligence, you have a miniscule chance to do that in today's mixed world. Such a world does not exist anymore and the only rare exceptions are found in extremely isolated societies.

Accept the world for what it is, a collaborative being of all of us together, similar and different in every way.

Cultures are groups of people of similar character, not actually people who are exactly the same. The more you understand and are prepared for that, the more success you will have in life - period.

Accept to serve the world as a whole and be served by the world as a whole. Stop dwelling on the differences and dwell on the similarities instead. It is that easy to create world peace, if we all understand this.

Within your own family, organization or society, you should be a leader of personal growth so as to improve individual characters, thereby improving the quality of the culture and its manifested collective outcome. Many different cultures have inspired or ruled most of the world throughout history. Each had its own contributions and shortfalls that led to its rise and demise.

"The time now calls for a global culture of singular focus and cohesive unity through acceptance, innovation, and service."

Throughout the existence of the Laser lifeCARE Institute, we have maintained one thing; a culture of mixed individuals that share a common purpose, to serve while innovating. Those who did not share or embrace the necessary character traits left the team and the team would come back into harmony. Through my leadership, our organizational culture remains diverse, yet united. Many times, new guests or colleagues have come into the Institute and remarked that it feels like the United Nations. I smile and affirm that we are more united than the United Nations.

Since the birth of the Laser lifeCARE Institute in New Zealand, we have had, and still have, the most diverse team imaginable, with members from Canada, the USA, Colombia, Puerto Rico, Brazil, Czech Republic, Germany, Slovakia, Hungary, Egypt, Sudan, South Africa, Palestine, Iran, India, Philippines, Australia, and, of course, some born and bred New Zealanders. Then there is me, and I am a global citizen.

This wonderful team includes members of both sexes, aligned with both sexual orientations, of different age groups, and different backgrounds. The spiritual beliefs range from atheist to Muslim, Catholic, Orthodox Christian, Anglican, Jewish, Seventh Day Adventist, Hindu, Sikh, and others. These are just the people who serve here, imagine the innumerable variations of the guests we serve.

The culture that we have created is that of cohesive characters that share the same traits. It is a corporate culture of excellence. Character-building of individual team members, chosen for their specific role, skills and attitude, happens from day one when they join the Laser lifeCARE Institute. Please visit us any time to experience it.

Imagine if all corporate entities, communities, societies, and nations accepted this as the new norm. Wouldn't this world become better and better?

"The world is becoming one, whether we like it or not. Let's make a choice to like it."

"Electing new country leaders cannot change the world. Electing to be a personal leader, taking charge of your own life, becoming better and inspiring others to do the same, is the way. That, my friend, is how you change the world."

Dr. Hisham Abdalla 2012

CHAPTER 6 NOTES

Watch Your Mouth

Watch your mouth, for whatever goes through, into or out of your mouth will affect your health, your life and others around you. These effects are physical, emotional, and mental. Watch your mouth, for it portrays who you are.

You did not think that you would get away without me talking about the mouth as a portal to your health and success, did you? I am a dentist and a doctor, after all.

So, let's take this further.

What goes into your mouth in terms of what you eat, drink, or consume will always determine your health and wellbeing. A healthy and radiant body is most critical for the expression of your leadership traits and for your longevity on this planet. I am not going to discuss diet and lifestyle in depth at this stage, as that will be the subject of my next book. For now, it is sufficient to point out the most obvious issues that face us in an abundant world, where excess is becoming the norm, not scarcity.

Excess in the consumption of all food, drinks, alcohol, and smoking is the main disease of the civilized world today. Moderation is the solution.

Please educate yourself and increase your awareness of what constitutes a good diet and lower your sugar and acid intake to minimum quantity and frequency. Alcohol, smoking, and drugs are the next most abused substances after food, sugar, and acidic drinks. Please limit your intake of all the above to be in better control of your health and life.

Don't let habits control you. You control your habits.

Don't use the term diet as a branded plan to lose weight. The word diet is being abused today as a temporary phase with magical powers on your health. Diet literally means nutrition and food. It should not be preceded by a brand or a fad name. Just decide to live on a good diet for life, with any occasional diversions being just that, momentary impulses of going off your path. Get back immediately on your chosen track of a good diet after such deviations. Diversions are normal if you are human, just recognize them, accept them, don't live in guilt, and move back to the path of moderation.

It is much more important for us as individuals and health professionals to study, promote, and seek health, attaining it and maintaining it, than it is to keep dwelling on disease.

Unfortunately, most health professionals are actually trained as disease management professionals and most people boast of their ailments much more than they talk about their wellness. That creates a mentality of seeking more negative attraction, even if we say that we don't want it.

What you talk about and dwell on, you will attract, regardless of what you are actually saying about it.

Let's raise our awareness and focus on what we want to attract (health) while overcoming the obstacles that we don't want (disease). That is my core health philosophy and motto.

"Let's seek health, rather than fight disease".

What goes on inside your mouth will affect your physical health and your attractiveness to the rest of the world. Controlling your oral health is most critical for your general health, wellness, attractiveness, and longevity. Bad Biofilm (bacteria cities) in your mouth will affect your teeth, gums, bone, and breath. They will also affect your heart, brain, kidneys, unborn child, spouse, and children. Those bad bugs travel throughout your body and pass from person to person through kissing. Bad breath is one of the most antisocial deterrents to other people looking to interact with you.

Invest a little time and effort every day to look after your mouth like you look after your other precious possessions and you will reap amazing benefits. Invest in proper, motivating dental health care and you should see and feel the difference.

Smile a lot. Use your facial expressions to impact positively on others, as they cannot avoid looking at and being influenced by your face, particularly your mouth, when you are communicating.

"A smile is the brand you wear on your face, for life. It says it all, without you saying a word, for it speaks to the soul of the world."

A smile is the core universal language that crosses barriers without sound, lyrics or effort. Even a baby will understand what a smile denotes, before they learn any other meaning in life. Desire the smile that will increase your confidence and influence, then get it and learn to keep it and use it.

Language used to communicate is as much physical and emotional as it is verbal. Body language speaks louder than words and impacts deeper.

People will remember how you made them feel for much longer than they would remember what you actually said. A cordial smile will leave an enduring impact.

What comes out of your mouth, literally and metaphorically, evidently has the ultimate impact on your life, leadership, and success. Words that you say to yourself or others, and thoughts that you metaphorically say, will have the largest impact on attracting, deterring, influencing or motivating yourself and people around you.

Speak well of yourself, with confidence and pride, but without conceit. Speak well of others, with praise and compliments, and without sleaze. Speaking well of fellow human beings attracts people of such character to you. You need such people on your side, on your team, and to desire your services.

Here are 7 of my most effective methods to engage and gain people support:

1. Find something about the person in front of you to compliment, and then say it.

2. Find things in common and talk about them. Find out about them by asking, and then listening. Talk about yourself only after the other person talks about themselves.

3. Do not put people down, abuse verbally or humiliate them with what you say or how you say it.

4. If a mistake is made, handle it as a situation that needs to be corrected, rather than criticizing the person for making a mistake. This is especially critical if someone has sought your professional help and advice.

Have empathy instead of sympathy. Feel with them, rather than sorry for them.

Sympathy ingrains "poor me" feelings and evokes a negative view of life. Empathy evolves care and engages one clear goal: How can I help make it better? That is being solution-oriented and gives hope.

5. Find solutions that provide the person involved with a way out that makes them aware that they have the responsibility and ability to change things.

6. Show people that you love them, but that you don't like their behavior or the problem that occurred due to their actions.

7. Be on their side when you help a person identify problems and discover solutions. If you blame the person directly or abuse them, you are disempowering them. If you empower them to correct their action and behavior, and support them in becoming better, then they may choose you as their leader.

Muhammad Ali's wisdom is portrayed again in his saying: "I wish people would love everybody else the way they love me. It would be a better world."

Apply courtesy every day to people around you. It does not matter whether they are less, more, or as fortunate as you. Applying courtesy in everyday life sets the stage for you to receive courtesy in return. Don't always expect immediate reward or payment; just give away some thing or some time every day. The rewards will come back to you multiplied. That is a universal law.

Improve your vocabulary all the time. Learn bits of other languages in order to better connect with other people. Learn to speak at least two languages.

The fact that I speak, read, and write three languages fluently (English, Arabic and Czech) and can somehow communicate within reason in French, Spanish, Italian, German, Slovak, Russian, Greek, Persian, and Hebrew, has given me huge advantages and influence in everyday interactions with people around the globe. I am not eloquent in all these languages, but I can understand a lot and repeat words with meaning to make a point and to engage.

Once people see that you are trying to learn their language, even if it is a few words, they will be more accepting of you and more likely to try to help you communicate with them. You don't have to be fluent in every language. The good news is that the more languages you learn, the better you can understand and learn other languages.

Most languages of different regions have common roots, like the Latin-based French, Spanish, and Italian. They are so similar in many ways that they can almost seem like different accents, rather than different languages sometimes. You will know what I mean if you try saying "how are you" and answer "good" in these three languages.

Aramaic, Arabic, and Hebrew are Semitic languages that have exactly the same roots, just like their people, and the three major religions of the world that originated in the one geographical region. They are all variations of the same. The first alphabet in all is Aleph, the writing is from right to left, and most words share the same origins. This makes it possible to understand many of them, once you learn one or the other. The word "alphabet" in English is actually derived from Semitic ABJAD and from Greek Alpha, Beta.

Talking about the shared origins of words and their meaning is actually an important point, especially if a person speaks only one language and has not been exposed to others.

For example, the Arabic word Allah (Al-Ilah) literally means "The One God" in English. It is used by all Arabic speaking people of different religions and denominations like Muslims, Catholics, Orthodox Christians, Anglicans, Copts, Assyrian Christians, Jewish and others; to denote the same God they all pray to. It is Eloah/Elohim in Hebrew and Elaha in Aramaic. Do they sound the same? Well, they are!

In Greek, Theos is the word for God, giving us the English word Theology. Every other language has its own word/s for God. They are not names; they are words of specific meaning pertinent to that language, regardless of religion, nationality or race.

I still wonder why people fight for power, money and land, but blame their religions and origins as the "Real Cause". The real cause of all human suffering is greed and deceit, because the other stuff is actually all the same, not different, if you care to understand.

For us to assimilate a global culture of unity, we have to understand, respect, and accept the differences between language, culture, religion, and nationality. They are all variations that affect people's views of the world, but they are also points of connection when we understand their similarities and how to integrate them to drive influence.

———————

Teach yourself, through the many means available today, to speak better and better in front of others. Whether you plan on giving presentations to one person or thousands of people at a time, you are always presenting and selling something to the person in front of you.

You are selling yourself at all times. You can only sell yourself by confidently communicating, with humility and dignity, to one person at a time, even if you are presenting to a room of ten thousand. People think and react as individuals, not as groups. Everyone in each group is a distinct individual who is processing what you are saying and how you're saying it, and then making a subconscious decision whether to accept you or not.

> Without selling you, you cannot sell
> your idea, service or product.

Selling is a two-way communication street. You offer, but the other person has to accept and decide to buy, otherwise it is not a sale. For that to happen, the key is communication. Good communication relies on good verbal, emotional, and physical expression of your idea, concept, and above all - you.

Selling is about building a relationship.

If you want to succeed in life and lead yourself, your family, and your organization or society, you have to continue making a good offer in a relationship, so your spouse, friend, customer or business associate continues to buy you.

Relationships built on a one time "amazing deal" are fads that don't last.

If you want people's love and admiration and lasting relationships, don't make yourself a "limited time special offer". Make yourself a continual "great value deal" that will always deliver, for as long as you live. Speak it, communicate it, and deliver it, then watch the others buy it: you.

It is your job to become better and better all the time. When everyone commits to improving himself or herself every day and in every way, then the world will definitely advance.

That is the only way to change the world for the better, one person at a time.

Personal leadership is the beginning of family, organizational, societal and World unity. Start with yourself, then influence and lead others to do the same. Look in the mirror and ask that person to make the change, before asking others to change.

As I wrote in the beginning of this book, people choose to be led by a person's character, integrity, achievement, and willingness to share.

Choose to be a 4D leader who inspires others.

Choose to be worthy of following.

Choose to live for a better meaning.

Find your legend and serve your time well on this earth, before you expect time to serve you.

Trust in the good of this world and great things will happen to all of us, together.

Yours in health and in peace

Dr. Hisham

CHAPTER 7 NOTES

"Let's make our time on this earth count. It's not the experiences we gain that matter, it's the ones that we share. To share more, you have to have more, be more and live more. Don't settle for a little, when abundance is your right and sharing is your duty. Live and leave a legend that shines."

Let's make our motto:

To Excellence and beyond, always better and better...

Dr. Hisham 2012

4D LEADERSHIP – INDEX EXCERPTS

Every evolution of an idea, innovation, or new reality was once a dream in some person's mind. The simple truth is that everything from attracting the relationships that you want, to earning more money, to leading a fulfilling life or inventing something and all the way to changing the world, starts with thoughts that become ideas that formalize into a dream. A dream is a mental vision of what could be.

Awareness is what determines our level of dreams. If you are not aware of your potential, ability, current situation, or level of vibration, how can you dream of more?

Dreams control your destiny, so make it a conscious choice to dream that destiny. Otherwise, it will be done for you by circumstance. One choice makes you a Victor, the other a Victim. Yet either way, you made a choice.

People forget many things, thankfully, but they will always remember how we made them feel. That flash memory happens as soon as we cross their mind or path again.

...human internal motivation is summarized in these two core emotional drivers: pain and pleasure. Everything we do is exclusively driven by our basic drive to attain pleasure or to avoid pain.

Applying the core emotional drivers of human behavior to our subject is something one must understand and master over time. Your desire and dream can only drive you if they are associated with attaining emotional pleasure. If they do not harmonize with your paradigms (habitual ways of thinking or core values) then the opposite will happen. That same noble desire and great dream will now cause you emotional pain. This means that no matter how much your conscious thoughts say: yes - go forward, your subconscious mind will say: NO, STOP RIGHT NOW, PAIN AHEAD.

This is the process of mental sabotage. This is the reason many people cannot give up addictive behavior even though they know very well that it is physically harming them and many actually want to stop, consciously. The subconscious mind will always dominate in our lives and its programming is our code.

...you have to be aware of how your current dreams and desires relate to your ingrained paradigms. That enables you to recognize whether they align or not and what to do about it. If the dream and desire are big enough and they collide with your paradigms, you will suffer immense emotional pain.

One of the two will have to change, either the dream or your paradigm. That is a choice only you can make and the responsibility is all on you.

Page 19

Pain avoidance is a much stronger emotional driver than pleasure seeking.

Page 21

Procrastination is the leading killer of dreams. Its antidote is the action verb: DO.

Page 25

Doing things in life randomly, without purpose and intent, is like driving your car around your whole life without a destination, until you run out of gas in the middle of nowhere.

Page 25

To quickly cut through the fourth dimension of time, it is much easier to pay for knowledge and learn through other people's mistakes and achievements in your chosen field or dream. This can help you avoid making the same mistakes and can give you a new platform from which to continue your rise upwards from their last level of achievement. Doing everything from scratch, without mentors and/or coaches, is not advisable if you want to reach a big goal fast.

"Learn from others so you can leverage your time of doing better. Then, share your doing so others can do better."

Page 30

Doing is participating with the Universe in making your desired dream a reality. Consistent participation leads to great results and success. Making the decision to only produce excellent results means that you have to unswervingly do things in an excellent manner.

A rule of happiness in life is to do what you love to do. If you are not living this rule, then you have two options: learn to love what you do or change what you are doing.

Determination... bends the dimension of time towards your result... time will not bend to serve you if you did not serve your time.

Leaders develop solutions to problems many times before the problems become eminent. Problem solving is important, but it is reactive. Active solution orientation is more ideal.

The determination to win should never be confused with competition to keep others out of the way. It should invigorate you and the people around you to all win - together.

11 Points to Success...

Character comes from within, the thoughts and beliefs that one holds in their mind make one's character.

Your character, based on your core values and thoughts, determines your paradigms and habits. A paradigm is a habitual way of thinking. That, in turn, determines your actions, which determine your outcomes. All this happens by choice, conscious or subconscious, not by default.

11 Character Traits of a Leader...

Excess in the consumption of food, drinks, alcohol, and smoking is the main disease of the civilized world today. Moderation is the solution.

It is much more important for us as individuals and health professionals to study, promote, and seek health, attaining it and maintaining it, than it is to keep dwelling on disease. Unfortunately, most health professionals are actually trained as disease management professionals...

A smile is the brand you wear on your face, for life. It says it all, without you saying a word, for it speaks to the soul of the world.

7 methods to Gain People Support...

Relationships built on a one time "amazing deal" are fads that don't last. If you want people's love and admiration and lasting relationships, don't make yourself a "limited time special offer". Make yourself a continual "great value deal" that will always deliver, for as long as you live. Speak it, communicate it and deliver it, then watch the others buy it: you.

ABOUT THE AUTHOR

Dr. Hisham Abdalla is founder of the Laser lifeCARE Institute and LaserKids Dental. He is the first multiple-laser dentist and instructor in New Zealand. He is an international speaker, author and educator in the fields of laser dentistry, high-tech, minimally invasive and cosmetic dentistry.

He is an innovator in the fields of Full Face Aesthetics, combining the arts of cosmetic dentistry and cosmetic medicine, and is one of very few dentists lecturing globally to cosmetic physicians, plastic surgeons and cosmetic experts, GP's, midwives and lactation consultants. He is an AUS/NZ course provider and examiner for The Queensland University Laser Safety Certification program and an affiliate member of the American Dental Association.

Dr. Hisham is a Fellow & Diplomate of the World Congress of Minimally Invasive Dentistry and had served as a directors' board member of the organization in the USA. He is a Founding member of the NZ Academy of Cosmetic Dentistry, Founding member & past VP of the NZ Institute of Minimal Intervention Dentistry, and Fellow of the World Clinical Laser Institute. He currently serves on the Advisory Board of Aesthetics Asia annual Congress in Singapore. He was an invited Associate Professor at the University of Cagliari in Italy.

Dr. Hisham is known for his pioneering ideas, strong motivation, and passion for research and sharing. His colleagues at the Auckland Dental Association nominated him for NZDA Young Dentist of the Year in 2005. In 2006, he represented NZ as the finalist at the Royal Australasian College of Dental Surgeons Young Lecturer of the Year Award in Sydney.

Dr. Hisham practices advanced dentistry and runs live courses for dental and medical professionals from all over the world, at the Professional Development Centre, at his Institute in Auckland. He graduated with honors from Charles University in Prague in 1998 as a Doctor of Dental Medicine (MUDR. of Stomatology) at age 21.

www.drhisham.co
www.4dleadership.com
www.lasersmile.co.nz
www.laserkidsdental.co.nz

Printed in Australia
AUOC011418021012
253961AU00001B/2/P